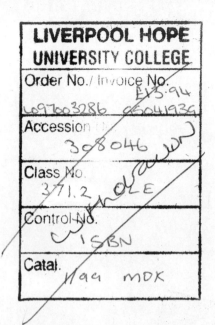

LEADING PRIMARY

SCHOOLS

LEADING PRIMARY
SCHOOLS

The pleasure, pain and principles of being a primary headteacher

DAVID CLEGG AND
SHIRLEY BILLINGTON

OPEN UNIVERSITY PRESS
Buckingham • Philadelphia

Open University Press
Celtic Court
22 Ballmoor
Buckingham
MK18 1XW

and
1900 Frost Road, Suite 101
Bristol, PA 19007, USA

First Published 1997

A catalogue record of this book is available from the British Library

ISBN 0 335 19645 4 (hbk)   0 335 19644 6 (pbk)

Library of Congress Cataloging-in-Publication Data
Clegg, David W.
    Leading primary schools : the pleasure, pain, and principles of
being a primary headteacher / David Clegg and Shirley Billington.
        p.   cm.
    Includes bibliographical references and index.
    ISBN 0–335–19645–4. — ISBN 0–335–19644–6 (pbk.)
    1. Elementary school principals—Great Britain.   2. School
management and organization—Great Britain.   I. Billington,
Shirley.   II. Title.
LB2831.926.G7C54   1997
372.12'012'0941—dc21   97–19367
                                                              CIP

Typeset by Graphicraft Typesetters Limited, Hong Kong
Printed in Great Britain by St Edmundsbury Press Ltd,
Bury St Edmunds, Suffolk

CONTENTS

INTRODUCTION

This book is for practising and aspiring primary headteachers. It is a modest attempt to reassert a view of primary headship which is rooted in reality rather than the mechanistic fantasy of managerialism. The book argues that any account of primary headship must confront values and attitudes before giving regard to a series of managerial competencies. It is, we believe, a timely book. The recent national initiative to construct a headteacher qualification offers an opportunity to reflect upon what the curriculum leading to the qualification might contain. We argue that being a primary headteacher is deeply personal and draws upon the reservoir of headteachers' attitudes and attributes, rather than being a mixture of abilities and skills. We believe that educational leadership should demonstrate particular characteristics which are grounded in educational philosophy rather than market economics. The book asserts that those involved in headteacher training must confront those characteristics and study in depth the implications they hold for the way our schools are run and, perhaps more importantly, how they develop and improve.

We have an opportunity to change the perspective of primary headship, to reassert the central importance of relationships within a school and to gain a fresh realistic perspective upon much of the unproven and unsubstantiated rhetoric of school management studies which place such importance upon tasks and competencies. We offer a view of school management which is not driven by effectiveness and efficiency but by ethics and morality.

We hope that this book will reassure the vast number of primary headteachers who day by day are confronted with the complexity of running a school, who know that change and development take time, who know that the system is overloaded yet still manage to enjoy being responsible for what happens. It may give them renewed confidence to resist the quick-fix merchants and those who argue that the way to improvement lies in systems, structures and documentation. It will, we hope, give them the confidence to follow their instincts, play a long game and demonstrate an enduring commitment to primary education by sustaining the professional development of all teachers.

1

THE PARADOX

OF HEADSHIP

Being a primary headteacher is complex, demanding and difficult. With education being very much in the public arena and a high profile debate being conducted on standards, teaching methods and test results, primary schools are very aware of and sensitive to the expectations placed on them by both legislation and the communities which they serve. These expectations, or even requirements, are frequently diverse and on occasions diametrically opposed. As a headteacher, you will be instrumental in trying to make sense and give coherence to the range of demands while at the same time endeavouring to ensure that you take colleagues, governors, parents, children and at times local politicians, officers and perhaps the media with you. With the political determination to 'open up education to the market place' (Department for Education and Employment (DFEE) official speaking of the introduction of the nursery voucher scheme in 1996), it would be difficult for even the most experienced headteacher to reconcile the laws of 'the market place' with values and principles which guide and influence fundamental aspects of the school's practice.

In this book, we explore the dilemmas with which primary headteachers are confronted on a daily and long-term basis. While no neat solutions are presented, we do offer some practical strategies to enable heads to steer a course through difficult waters. We provide a particular and distinct view of primary headship which is centrally concerned with values and attitudes. We argue that as a headteacher you should demonstrate these values and attitudes in all aspects of your role, but particularly through the relationships you form with all those with whom you work. In recent years, in-service training, inspection and research have been particularly concerned with the managerial aspects of headship. While we recognize the need to

ensure that a school is effectively managed, we take issue with
some aspects of current management orthodoxy and particularly
with the competency-based approach to headship. There is, in our
view, a distinction between seeing the role of a headteacher as a
series of disconnected and atomized skills and *being* a headteacher,
which implies a personal commitment within a specific context.

Undertaking a professional role and investing commitment at a personal level are clearly interlinked and, as we shall argue later, there
may well be particular personal qualities and skills which a headteacher needs. Indeed, it could be asserted that there has always
been a personal dimension to headship, in that headteachers have
been expected to demonstrate and reflect the values which a society
places on its primary education system. The expectations that headteachers would be models for both other teachers and pupils were
very clear in the first seventy years of primary education.

The role of the headteacher in the late nineteenth and early
twentieth centuries was that of day-to-day responsibility for educational and moral leadership, acting under the direction of the school
managers. The term 'headteacher' was synonymous with that of
'leading teacher', so that the head would be the senior teacher, usually teaching the oldest group of pupils, as well as the supervisor of
other teachers. Successful Victorian headteachers, or headmasters as
they almost always were, were renowned for their strong discipline.
They ensured an adherence to rigid routines, supervised teachers
and pupils closely and exercised strong sanctions against those who
stepped out of line, in the form of physical punishment for pupils,
and teachers on occasions, and instant dismissal of unsatisfactory
staff. A well managed school was a well regimented school, and
the power invested in the position is clearly demonstrated by the
headmaster Edward Thring who is quoted as saying in 1926: 'I am
supreme here and will brook no interference' (Peters 1976).

Being headteacher in the local elementary school provided the
opportunity to exert a degree of social control, ensuring that established values and understanding were transmitted through education.
Since leadership in education necessitated being an exemplar of
particular religious and moral beliefs, headteachers were required
to perpetrate these beliefs through the role they assumed in the
community as well as through the way they ran their schools. The
concept of education as a form of social control preserving class
cultures continued well into the twentieth century, indeed into the
1930s, but the dramatic effect of the Second World War, in terms of
changing established roles in society, also impacted on the provision
of education and led to new concepts of educational leadership and

responsibility. Plans to develop a socially equitable and democratic society, or in other words 'Building a Better Britain', were based on the premise that education was the means to achieve this end.

'Building a Better Britain' meant ensuring opportunities for more people to have greater participation in decision-making, increasing productivity through modernizing systems and developing high-quality services and support structures which could be available to all citizens. Education had a key role to play if this was to be achieved. The post-war period, therefore, saw a shift in the perception of education as a method of preserving the status quo in society to education as a means to create opportunities for improvement. Rather than importing a given set of established values and providing a basis in the three Rs, education was to be the means of developing each individual's capacity for learning; ensuring that each reached his or her potential. The Labour government regarded education as a vehicle for breaking down class barriers and long-established hierarchical structures. Education was a responsibility of the state and an entitlement for all citizens. The type of leader needed for a school was different, therefore, to the Victorian headmaster conscious of his position and eager to ensure that pupils knew their place. If education was to be a public service, rather than a form of benevolent provision, then the state would have a key role as provider and in particular as provider of appropriate funding for expansion. The leaders of schools which were to open up a range of opportunities to future citizens needed a social conscience and a view of what education might achieve. In addition to being the leading teacher, the headteacher was also expected to be, to some extent, an agent of social change. The increase in the role and responsibilities of the state for education created the potential for a head to establish a degree of individuality about his or her school. If education were to become a genuine vehicle of opportunity, then it was desirable for a headteacher to have a professional identity and a set of beliefs about education, as well as skills of leadership and control.

The broadening of the aim of education to include a concern with pupils' personal development, and in particular with pupils as individuals rather than an homogeneous group, created opportunities for headteachers to make individual decisions about the organization of their schools. The group of teachers who moved up the career ladder and began to emerge as headteachers themselves during the 1960s were still very much 'super-teachers', but their approaches to teaching and learning might be regarded as innovative and liberating, and certainly questioned some of the established practices of the 1940s and 1950s in primary schools. 'The new head will have opposed streaming, corporal punishment, eleven plus education, single sex education, insulation from parents, the prefect system (unless elective), traditional examinations, didactic or even expository class teaching' (Musgrove, quoted in Grace 1995). The set of beliefs which were prescribed for and enacted by the Victorian head were replaced by new values related to sociological, cultural and pedagogic reform.

As the new generation of headteachers emerged, there was an increasing shift of power in institutional and professional terms, particularly in relation to school managers. While, in most cases, formal control of a school remained with the managers, practical leadership of a school and considerable power of decision-making rested with the headteacher. The position of headteachers was enhanced and empowered as never before, and they were therefore able to establish a large degree of professional autonomy which became embodied in the term 'my school'. The use of the possessive adjective indicates the degree of personal commitment which many headteachers invested in their work as well as the opportunity to demonstrate their personal and professional values through the way their schools were run: 'when headteachers of this period used the expression "my school" they were articulating a degree of manifest school leadership which was exceptional both historically and comparatively' (Grace 1995).

Headteachers were able to function from a position of considerable strength. Where managers did exist, they were rarely the landed gentry or the rich benevolent autocrats of the late nineteenth or early twentieth centuries, but were a combination of locally nominated representatives with a range of interests and backgrounds. Still generally drawn from the middle classes, many had professional occupations and a good number were themselves retired headteachers. A fundamental shift in the relationship between managers and headteachers compared to that which prevailed in the 1920s and 1930s was that the head was usually of equal, if not superior, status to the managers. The headteacher was clearly established as the leading professional and as the manifest school leader, with immense power in cultural, pedagogic and curriculum terms. For many teachers, therefore, the prospect of leadership was highly desirable, as it held the possibility of 'his' or 'her school' becoming 'my school'. Headship in primary schools held great potential for those wishing to activate change, although it would be a fundamental misrepresentation of the situation in schools to assume that all heads were engaged in revolutionizing the educational system. While a number of schools embodied new methods and introduced team teaching, family grouping and discovery learning, often in open-plan buildings, there were plenty of others which could be described as very traditional in approach and methodology.

Whatever the type of school, the point is that, during the 1960s and 1970s, headteachers were in a position as never before to make schools their own. If they chose to offer a narrow curriculum delivered in neat timetabled slots that was their prerogative, as much as it was the right of other heads to choose a more *laissez-faire* approach to the curriculum in which the work covered could develop from the interest of the child. In general terms, Coulson's (1974) argument that headteachers had great latitude in administering and organizing schools according to their own convictions is borne out by the variations in curriculum and pedagogy which could be found in a sample group of primary schools situated in the same area. Headteachers functioned with a blend of personal control and moral authority founded on the head's very personal identification with and sense of responsibility for, the school.

The degree of power invested in primary headteachers at that time was focused on the development of an individual school's culture, curriculum and pedagogy. The headteacher's role in management was very much an administrative one, concerned with the day-to-day organization and running of a school. There were considerable constraints in these areas, in that matters of financial control, staffing, resourcing and allocation of pupils to schools were the province of the local education authority. Headteachers had to operate within these constraints and the notion of management autonomy for schools was alien to the state sector. While this division of power and responsibility between the headteacher and the local education authority (LEA) was generally clear, it was not a situation which satisfied a number of influential groups or individuals.

The first Black Paper published in 1969 reflected a range of concerns about the education system, including the introduction of the comprehensive system, the student revolutions in the late 1960s and an analysis of standards of achievement in schools, with some apparently worrying evidence. This opened the floodgates for a number of largely right-wing groups and individuals to question the perceived autonomy of schools. Simultaneously, employers were raising a series of concerns about students' preparedness for work and urging the need to monitor standards of achievement. It was becoming increasingly apparent that public interest in a public service which was costing £6 billion annually was quite justifiable.

The Ruskin speech by the Prime Minister James Callaghan in 1976 cited 'legitimate public concern' which needed to be aired and to have 'shortcomings righted or put to rest'. One part of his speech heralded the dramatic change in curriculum organization which was to result in the introduction of the National Curriculum. 'It is not my intention to become enmeshed in such problems as whether there should be a basic curriculum with universal standards – although I am inclined to think that there should be' (Callaghan 1976). For the first time it seemed that what was taught in schools might be the legitimate concern of those outside the education system. Callaghan cited 'the unease felt by parents and teachers about the new informal methods of teaching which seem to produce excellent results when they are in well-qualified hands but are much more dubious in their effect when they are not.' The autonomy of the headteacher in deciding curriculum issues was at the beginning of the end.

As Callaghan was articulating concerns about the 'secret garden'of the curriculum, others were expressing the view that there was an imbalance of power embodied in the role of headteachers. Musgrove (quoted in Grace 1995) argued that they had considerable autonomy in cultural, professional and pedagogical aspects of their work but were disempowered in management. He suggested that heads needed to be in a position to make decisions about financial, staffing and resource issues if schools were to be genuinely autonomous: 'they [headteachers] have no voice in the major issues which concern their schools . . . they have no say in matters of finance and resources and recruitment of personnel' (Musgrove, quoted in Grace 1995). Musgrove identified a need for headteachers to have more power, particularly in budgetary matters, since 'financial control is at the heart of the managerial process'. His work preceded that of several others who pursued similar themes of headteachers as managers of individual institutions, and was also a precedent for the introduction in the 1990s of delegated budgets to schools. So here is one of the paradoxes of headship, in that, while the autonomy of headteachers in deciding curriculum issues was slipping away, their role in making management decisions was being enhanced.

It has also been argued (Grace 1995) that the development and expansion of the comprehensive system in the 1970s had an important impact on the nature of leadership in all types of schools. The sheer size and complexity of new or amalgamated comprehensive schools gave rise to the development of a new management culture. The appointment of headteachers was to depend in part on their management skills, rather than purely on their professional teaching expertise and personal commitment.

By the early 1980s headteachers were in a situation in which their jobs were becoming blurred. They were no longer in a situation in which they could determine the nature and organization of 'their curriculum'. At the same time they were taking on new responsibilities which many felt were far removed from their initial reasons for taking on headship, namely an interest in and concern for matters of teaching and learning. Southworth (1995) expresses very clearly a headteacher's concerns about the introduction of National Curriculum and local management of schools (LMS).

> [National Curriculum and LMS] are going to change the way I do my job because the job is changing. I don't happen to believe that it's a particularly good way, I don't happen to believe that it equates easily with the type of learning and teaching I would like to see happen in the school. I don't feel that there are many occasions when I can view the demands with enthusiasm, knowing that it's going to be clearly beneficial to teachers and children.
> (Quote from Ron Lacey, the subject of Southworth's book)

Southworth (1995) comments that this particular headteacher 'did not enjoy the prospect of headship becoming, as he saw it, preoccupied with administration and accountancy' (Southworth 1995).

Other reforms being considered by the Department of Education and Science (DES) during this period reflected the desire to open up the education system to the spirit of competition and market forces. Sir Keith Joseph's scheme to introduce education vouchers was to be the device which would radically alter the balance of power and relationships in education. By giving parents the opportunity to influence the provision of resources in schools through choosing where to spend their vouchers, standards in education would rise to satisfy these consumers. Although the voucher scheme had to be abandoned, largely because it proved to be too expensive to administer, the basis of the scheme as the means to exercise market forces still had considerable appeal to influential right-wing politicians and academics. The basis of their economic theory was that it would be more efficient to give the power of choice to the consumer rather than the provider, an approach applied as enthusiastically to health services as to the education system. Although the voucher system itself was not to be at that time, the notion of choice and market forces underpinned many subsequent reforms. The introduction of per capita funding, which is the basis of LMS schemes, the establishment of grant-maintained schools and open enrolment resulted in headteachers needing to be very aware of the means by which they were to attract and retain pupils. The language of reform inherent in recent legislation, policy and political commentary from the New Right illustrates very clearly the desire to ensure that schools assumed a provider–client relationship with parents. 'Schools will be forced by the market to provide a swift response to the wishes of parents' (Nicholas Bennett in Craig 1989), and

> if all existing maintained schools were to be deprived of their present monopoly privileges and thus become individual firms subject to the incentives and disciplines of the market . . . reliable measures of the teaching effectiveness at all levels of these schools would be rapidly evolved and publicised. For everybody knows that firms competing to sell their products strive to demonstrate the quality of those products to possible purchasers.
> (Fleur, quoted in Grace 1995)

The notion of teachers as 'deliverers' of the curriculum, parents as 'consumers', children as 'clients' and the school's accountability for measurable outcomes are all symptomatic of the development of a market-oriented consumerist system. Within this system schools are expected to reflect the simplistic notions of a materialistic society in which only that which can be measured is of real consequence. The climate in which headteachers of the late 1980s and early 1990s were to find themselves working is perhaps neatly summarized by Barnes (1993): 'The Education Reform Act 1988 promotes a market driven education system in which individual schools will need to sell their product in a competitive environment. The Education (Schools) Act 1992 will further intensify competition. This requires all schools to publish their public examination results including the SAT results for Key Stages 1, 2 and 3.'

While the responsibilities of headteachers as school administrators have been made clear through the articulation of management competences expected of them, their role in curriculum matters has not been ignored. The report *Curriculum Organisation and Classroom Practice in Primary Schools* (DES 1992) devotes an entire section to the headteacher's role in curriculum leadership, but sees this as being concerned with quality control and management rather than being an innovator or initiator of educational development. The role of the head in ensuring the quality of what is 'delivered' runs through the section: 'headship is leadership in quality assurance and assessment . . . plans, teaching methods, classroom organisation, work in progress and work completed all require monitoring on a regular basis . . . the information gathered through monitoring must then be evaluated in order to test aspirations against realities' (DES 1992). A series of questions then focus on specific aspects of the headteacher's role: 'How well does the work being undertaken reflect National Curriculum attainment targets and programmes of study? How far do the standards achieved reflect National Curriculum levels? How far does classroom practice reflect agreed whole school policies? What is the quality of planning, assessment and organisation?' (DES 1992).

More recently, the annual report of Her Majesty's Chief Inspector on Standards and Quality in Education (1995) is critical of the limited degree to which headteachers are monitoring the school's curriculum. 'Relatively few headteachers . . . spend sufficient time evaluating the quality of teaching and learning. Many should play a stronger part in curriculum development and, in particular, should review the implementation of new initiatives to ensure that the original objectives are being achieved' (Ofsted 1994). Despite the acknowledgement of the developmental aspect of a head's role, it is the headteacher's responsibility as monitor which is constantly expressed. The vast range of statutory requirements for curriculum and assessment ensures that there is a great deal to cross-check and potentially little time to reflect, analyse and create. A curriculum vision is fine, provided that it meets National Curriculum requirements and can be achieved within existing resources.

The dramatic shift in society's expectations of education, the development of legislation which has purported to bring about schools' autonomy while creating a straitjacket within which they must operate and the impact of subjecting education to market forces has created a series of dilemmas for headteachers. Society's expectations of schools, fuelled by media hype about falling standards and incompetent teachers, together with the political will to ensure public accountability, cannot be ignored. In this context, clearly being the 'super classroom teacher' of the 1960s in order to be a primary school head in the 1970s is no longer appropriate. At the same time, the majority of headteachers will want to resist the notion of the managerial aspect of headship being their prime function.

Increasingly headship is being equated to particular skills and competences which can be identified and assessed. There is a plethora of management courses for headteachers, often leading to accreditation, and recent proposals from the Teacher Training Agency (TTA) for the induction of new headteachers are again based on the development of management skills. Within such schemes, there is little acknowledgement of the intangible aspects of headship related to a headteacher's professional values and vision. The capacity to become a headteacher can be demonstrated through career advancement, which brings increasing responsibility to a teacher who becomes a senior member of staff and then a deputy, coupled with appropriate training to enable an individual to cope with a very complex and demanding role. As we said above, there is, however, a fundamental difference between taking on the role of headteacher and being a headteacher. Southworth (1995) in his study of Ron Lacey demonstrates very clearly that Ron's day-to-day work as a head was dependent on a set of beliefs and values which permeated many aspects of school life. The personal aspect of the role was interdependent with his professional identity and the implications of this are highlighted throughout the case study.

> Ron saw headship as a personal activity. It entailed the projection and enactment of *his* educational beliefs. Headship was always with him. It filled his head so that the school resided in a nerve, inside the head's head!
>
> Headship was not a job, it was a way of life. It was the integration of professional and personal beliefs and experience which were not so much worked out as *lived out* in the school . . .
>
> [He] carried headship with him because it was him. He had become a head and, in some senses, headship had become him.
>
> (Southworth 1995)

As Ron himself identified, however, the demands of 'feeling the role' were becoming increasingly complex in the late 1980s. Ron's work as a headteacher was being impeded by rapid changes in legislation and he was feeling the loss of the 'primacy of personal contact' (Fullan 1991) in effecting development in curriculum and pedagogy.

This decade has brought immense difficulties for those headteachers who wish to 'feel the role'. There is a genuine paradox in maintaining a sense of purpose and a personal definition of primary headship in an era which is characterized by demands to fulfil statutory requirements, to meet deadlines for a wide range of information, much of it to be made publicly available, and to maintain a positive image of the school which is necessary for its survival. What follows is an attempt to address this paradox by exploring some fundamental aspects of the primary headteacher's work, but first we need to investigate the reasons for some aspects of management training failing to provide an adequate account of the realities of the job.

2

THE MYTH OF THE

MANAGER

> We only have the vaguest idea of any but
> the most direct consequences of our acts ...
> our knowledge of the future is fluctuating,
> vague and uncertain.
>
> (Keynes, quoted by Hutton 1995)

We live in the age of the manager. Most of us engaged in the world
of education operate within some kind of management structure in
which duties, roles and responsibilities are allocated to individuals
according to their particular positions within the organization. So
pervasive has managerialism become that when the history of late
twentieth-century education is written it will have to account for
the proliferation of the ideas embedded within the curriculum
vitae of educational management studies. While the growth of such
studies has its origins in the increased size of secondary schools
during the 1960s, it has enjoyed increased prominence throughout
the educational reforms of the 1980s, which has resulted in the
marketization of the education service and the centralization of
educational decision-making. The hegemony of managerialism is
attested to by the vocabulary we now use to talk and write about
schooling. Schools must aim for efficiency and effectiveness, the
curriculum must be delivered, achievement must be monitored and
measured, staff must be appraised, plans must be drawn up and
schools must compete in the market place. This is the vocabulary of
modern day education as spoken by the management consultants
and the civil service bureaucrats. The ideas and vocabulary of managerialism have proved to be a potent mixture and have successfully
pervaded most aspects of education, but not without producing
significant tensions along the way. In some respects, as the forces of

managerialism and marketization gather pace, so the cracks begin to widen and the antagonism inherent in imposing one set of values and attitudes from corporate business institutions on to public service institutions framed within a completely different set of values is increasingly exposed.

It is not only education which has been subjected to the onslaught. Public services in general have felt the impact of marketization and the consequent intrusion of management. The National Health Service (NHS) has seen an enormous rise in the number of people who manage the system without a similar rise in the number of doctors and nurses (*The Guardian* 26 August 1995). Local government has been subjected to the ethos of competitive tendering and has to sell its services to the lowest bidder. The British Broadcasting Corporation (BBC) has also felt the deadening hand of management at the expense of programme makers. A common feature of those services and institutions which have been subjected to the onslaught of the management consultant appears to be a significant increase in the number of people who run an organization without an accompanying increase in the number of people who actually provide the service for which the institution was set up in the first place. At the BBC, there is an increasing number of people described by Janet Street-Porter (1995) as the 'dreaded Four M's: male, middle class, middle aged and mediocre', who are concerned with managing the organization, but not with actually making television or radio programmes. Street-Porter went on to claim that it is 'in the management of British Television that TV is a business where you pay more attention to the delivery mechanism than to the product which will actually drive it'. In other words, a frequent and familiar consequence of the growth of management is a subsequent diminishing of those activities which inform and demonstrate the original purposes of the organization. At the very least, resources are directed away from front-line services towards feeding the management appetite for facts, figures and measured outcomes.

Despite management claims to objectivity in pursuit of efficiency, the rhetoric of the New Right is a determined and ideological onslaught upon many of the values which have underpinned public service. The starting point for the New Right is that public services are inefficient and unsuccessful, and have failed their constituents. Whether this is or is not true is debatable, but owing to the idiosyncratic British system of democracy, what is increasingly debarred from debate is an open discussion of possible solutions. Hence we see in the NHS the use of gagging clauses in employees contracts, which debar them from making public criticism of what is a public service!

The rampant ideologically blinkered response is to thrust the public service into the market place, where a cold blast of reality is meant to shock institutions out of the cosy world of parents, patients and pupils into the real world of contractors, clients and consumers. What is happening to our public services is therefore a battle of ideas and what is happening in our schools is a battle for the hearts and minds of headteachers. The battleground has been careful prepared. The starting point for the new right has been the apparent failure of our education system and this failure has been used to legitimize the 'discourse of derision' to which teachers have been subjected over the past few years. What has happened is a deliberate attempt to drive a wedge between parents and schools to generate a climate of mistrust between those who provide the service and those who receive it.

It is not a scenario which encourages optimism. Janet Street-Porter remarks that the assumption being made about the BBC is that it is 'unwell' and needs a dose of management! It (the BBC) is to be cured by a new wave of company doctors brought in to run the business with their management consultants, flow charts, overhead projectors and objectives which become the daily prescription for recovery (*The Guardian* 26 August 1995). As far as schools and teachers are concerned, Inglis (1989) sums up the cynicism and anger felt by many of those who have been on the receiving end of the narrow ideology of management masquerading as common sense:

> glancing down the titles of the contributors to administrative primers, at the list of in-service courses in local authority offices or University Schools of Education, the regulatory terminology reporting the vocabulary of contemporary oppression, the inscription of the omnipresent techniques of surveillance and incarceration upon the harmless lives of classrooms, libraries, playing fields, school outings, camp. The currency of accountability, bureaucratic rationality, professionality can only be cashed at state banks. It is simply not convertible into what one innocently thinks of as the real values of education.

This bleak view of managerialism is not mere name calling; it is to argue that managerialism is unable to engage with those issues which are the central concerns of education. Those who associate themselves with managerialism, the managers and administrators, together with the consultants and gurus, make considerable claims about the benefits of systems and structures. We wish to argue with some of the assumptions behind managerialism and show that it is incapable of providing the solutions it claims, and it is an inappropriate model through which to explore the job of the headteacher.

Managerialism, and the subsequent growth of complementary school management studies, results from the fact that educational administration is, to a large extent 'informed by the assumptions of bureaucratic rationality' (Rivzi 1989). Bureaucratic rationality is the form of organization articulated by Max Weber around the turn of the century. It is characterized by legal rules, clearly defined separate functions, authority of office rather than the person and detailed records. To Weber, bureaucracy was the most rational way of organizing to achieve efficiency. It is based largely upon the belief that the establishment of organizations can be subjected to scientific reason and that bureaucracy is the rational way to ensure an organization's efficiency. It is important to understand that Weber's view of rationality makes the key assumptions that statements of fact and judgements of value are logically distinct, and that scientific rationality is only concerned with statements of fact. The other side of this coin means that Weber maintains that judgements of value cannot be arrived at rationally because in the final analysis they are personal likes, dislikes, preferences or attitudes. In other words, what is being promulgated is that the means by which an organization achieves efficiency can be decided by rational argument, but the ends to which the organization is committed cannot.

The impact of this is made very clear by Rizvi: 'Modern administrative theory is fundamentally embedded within the framework of this Weberian view of rationality. It systematically eschews making judgements on the morality of organisational ends, for it rests on the assumptions that ends cannot be subjected to the scrutiny of reason' (Rizvi 1989). It is Weber's contention that bureaucracy is only concerned with means, and by definition cannot be concerned with ends. It is this apparent separation of means and ends which allows managers to make claims of neutrality and objectivity. Seen in this light, the headteacher simply has to create an organization or bureaucracy which is most efficient and effective in delivering the National Curriculum. The central concern becomes the means, completely divorced from the ends. If we consider this further, we can begin to understand how school management studies have been given their legitimacy. If the ends, in the shape of the National Curriculum, have already been decided, then the headteacher's job is to devise the most efficient means to obtain the ends. In other words, the organization essentially becomes an end in itself. The results of this thinking are plain to see in the contemporary arguments about many of our public services. The emphasis upon creating an effective school or an efficient hospital actually gets in the way of discussions about what are the purposes of schools and hospitals.

It is in fact the basis of school management studies to consider means rather than ends: hence the emphasis upon the senior management team and staffing structures, school development planning, action planning and the constant need to be able to demonstrate and illustrate the apparent efficiency of the organization. This need to demonstrate efficiency, or to be accountable in current terminology, brings its own particular madness into the system. As we have said, accountability has been reduced to a crude set of limited figures which relate only to those aspects of the system amenable to measurement, and the corollary of this has meant that if it cannot be measured it is not important. As one IBM executive put it, 'measurement is the heart of any improvement process. If something cannot be measured, it cannot be improved' (Peters 1989). The ludicrous result of this point of view is the dubious and uncomfortable task given to Ofsted inspectors of grading pupils' spiritual, moral, cultural and social development. The fact is, that as our education system becomes increasingly centralized, those at the centre require more bureaucracy and, more importantly, they look to develop the features and characteristics of bureaucratic rationality. The results of this thinking can be seen in many different aspects of the education service generally and the view of headship in particular. The whole thrust of management development studies has been to sharpen headteachers' skills and techniques which will enable them to create the means for the efficient and effective delivering of the centrally imposed curriculum and assessment arrangements.

The most recent example of this thinking can be seen in the arrangements for the Headteachers' Leadership and Management Programme (HEADLAMP) proposed by the TTA. This is a national scheme designed to provide management training for newly appointed headteachers. In the original consultation document the proposed training requirements referred to 'managerial tasks and competencies' which reflected most of the elements catalogued in management development courses, despite the concerns being raised about the adequacy of competency-based training. The assumptions behind the proposed tasks and competencies were again those of bureaucratic rationality: the need to identify strategic goals, careful planning and the monitoring of teachers' and pupils' performances. The boundaries of action open to headteachers were clearly demarcated within these proposals. As a result of the consultation exercise, the reference to competencies was dropped and the term abilities was substituted, but the assumptions remained. This technicist, atomized view of the job of being a headteacher does not reflect realities and fails to provide an adequate frame of reference within which the real issues of leadership in education and schooling can be explored. To view the job simply in terms of tasks, abilities or competencies renders the actual job meaningless, in that it suggests that the various tasks and abilities are somehow independent of the setting or milieu in which they take place. Without some understanding of the context, actions such as headteachers using their abilities to fulfil their tasks become unintelligible. As McIntyre says, 'we cannot characterise behaviour independent of intention and we cannot characterise intention independently of the settings' (McIntyre 1985). In other words, what individual headteachers do only really makes sense within the context of their individual schools and, furthermore, what they do will be dependent upon the particular circumstances of their schools. We can illustrate this through example. A particular task identified by the TTA as a key aspect of a headteacher's job is 'assessing and reviewing standards of pupils' achievement and the quality of teaching and learning'. While many headteachers may not disagree with this being an aspect of their job, the ways in which they approach it may be very different. Before beginning to tackle this, you would need to know in some detail the context within which you are working. Decisions would have to be taken about some very fundamental and value-laden issues, such as 'What is it important to assess achievement in?' or 'What part should pupils play in the assessment process?' It would also be important to have an awareness of other factors, such as 'What is the school's current approach?', 'Is there a history of testing?' or 'What do parents expect?' It is only through answering these questions and others of similar ilk that you can begin to make decisions and embark on a course of action which makes sense.

The above example is also useful in that it demonstrates the difficulties of separating ends and means. If we look at some of the questions above about assessment of achievement, we can see that to answer these questions is to engage with issues essentially concerned with values and attitudes. To ask what is to be assessed is also to ask what is important; the level of participation of pupils in their own assessment will inevitably go to the heart of attitudes concerned with pupils' learning and parental expectations will vary according to their particular attitudes. Indeed, the importance that the school attaches to assessment and how it is managed will inevitably involve discussions about purposes and priorities. In other words, how a school might set about addressing the issues surrounding assessment will involve some fundamental discussion about the purposes of schooling which will be essentially concerned with values and attitudes.

As we noted earlier, the problem for bureaucratic rationality and the management studies curriculum it has spawned is that it is incapable of engaging with ends, as it denies their susceptibility to be arrived at rationally. In this sense, the management studies curriculum has very clear boundaries, and suffers from what Ferguson (1984) refers to as radical deafness. It is essentially hostile to many of the usual concerns of political, social and educational theory. The questions with which bureaucratic rationality and management studies are concerned focus upon systems and routines and do not engage with the wider issues of value and attitudes. Indeed, the disappearance from the National Curriculum of the cross-curricular themes and dimensions, and hence those areas concerned with the environment, multicultural education and citizenship, may well have been a result of 'radical deafness'. We remain in the perennial discussion of how best to 'deliver the curriculum'.

We can see how bureaucratic rationality, and its impact upon educational administration, denies access to any discussion about educational values. As we have seen in the earlier example, however, the determined separation of means and ends is not tenable: what we wish to assess cannot be separated from how we wish to assess. If we desire to teach children to be independent, questioning and democratic, three unfashionable but legitimate aims, then how we teach them and what we assess become a fundamental issue. If a headteacher wants the school to be a genuine living expression of the values, attitudes and aspirations of all the teaching staff, and the community the school serves, then that has clear implications for how the school is run. What we are arguing for here is that since the curriculum of current management studies is limited by the Weberian model of bureaucratic rationality, by its own definition it is incapable of engaging in discussion about educational values.

There are other claims made on behalf of management studies which need to be looked at to establish further the invalidity of some of its aspirations, and indeed to demonstrate that current management training fails to provide a coherent view of educational administration. To achieve this we need to explore two further aspects of bureaucratic rationality: first, its claim to be neutral, objective and indeed rational; second, the knowledge the manager claims to possess to fulfil his or her tasks.

If we refer back to some of the characteristics of bureaucratic rationality, the particular emphasis upon skills, techniques, systems and structures forms a major part of management's claim to rationality, in that the deployment of these attributes is neutral and objective. Bureaucratic rationality displaces the language of values, politics and morals with those of efficiency and effectiveness. Since the language of administration is presented as neutral, it is unable to make a distinction between those relationships which are based upon manipulation and those of a non-manipulative nature, since all relationships are based on the premise of achieving efficiency and effectiveness. As McIntyre (1985) shows, administration is 'Lacking any uniform or even inter-subjective criteria for the judgement of moral ends, human relationships – become a matter of persons treating each other as a means to their ends.' Taking this further we can ask the question: what is the morality of individuals trying to influence and persuade people to work to achieve others' ends? Is this what we want pupils to learn?

A consequence of the manager's claim to neutrality and objectivity is the degree to which bureaucracy is concerned to depersonalize working relationships by ensuring that the activities with which individuals engage are directed to predetermined ends, and to an increasing extent bureaucracy organizes formal structures within which individuals engage with each other. What this leads to is the formality of various meetings, with predetermined agendas, perhaps best demonstrated by the convoluted system of teacher appraisal in which the meetings have written rules of engagement. This is a long way from the notion of people meeting to talk about what they're doing! Of course all this procedure is an attempt to iron out the difficulties of working relationships and personality clashes, and to avoid conflict: 'Nothing personal you understand but . . .' The question, however, is whether this claim to neutrality and objectivity can be sustained. On the surface, claims of achieving efficiency and effectiveness sound entirely reasonable, particularly if we consider their opposite. No one wants to be considered as inefficient or ineffective, and certainly in the past few years teachers and schools have been cajoled and bullied into seeing efficiency and effectiveness as the two prizes to be won. We only have to look at the Ofsted Framework for Inspection to understand the status accorded to efficiency, and no one in the teaching profession can be unaware of the emphasis upon effectiveness and the ubiquitous effective schools movement. However, we have seen how ends and means are not amenable to being separated, and therefore the manager who claims to be concerned only with means is inevitably implicated in the ends. The claim to neutrality is spurious, both from the point of view that ends are closely linked with means and that efficiency and effectiveness are not neutral or unproblematic concepts. Both efficiency and effectiveness are tricky ideas, but neither can lay claim to being what Rizvi (1989) refers to as 'an ideal which is self-evidently worth pursuing'. It is worth bearing in mind that vast geographical areas of Britain have been reduced to poverty and social disintegration in the name of efficiency. In coming to terms with notions of efficiency, we have to ask: efficient for whom? Efficient in what terms? For example, should we prize efficiency over participation? In other words, the notion of efficiency is not value free. It carries with it implications and assumptions which we can either accept or reject. The current hegemony would point to efficiency as a universal good, but then as Andrew Marr wryly observes, 'Efficiency has always been emblazoned on the black flag of the centralist' (Marr 1995).

The notion of effectiveness is equally problematical. It sits comfortably with bureaucratic rationality since the purpose of the bureaucracy is to achieve the stated aims effectively, but in fact the whole notion of effectiveness is associated with a 'mode of human existence in which the contrivance of means is in central part the manipulation of human beings into compliant patterns of behaviour' (McIntyre 1985). In other words, effectiveness, in managerial terms, is synonymous with getting people to do what you wish them to do, essentially, as noted above, treating people as means rather than ends. We can, therefore, have some regard to the morally dubious nature of managerial effectiveness, but there is another, perhaps more immediate and compelling critique of the claims of managerial effectiveness. To be able to sustain the idea of management effectiveness, managers have to lay claim to particular information and knowledge, which McIntyre refers to as managerial and bureaucratic expertise, to enable them to achieve effectiveness in their own terms.

The entire premise of managerial effectiveness rests on two notions. The first is that management is objective and morally neutral, but as we have seen this is a chimera, as the idea of effectiveness is only meaningful in terms of ends, and ends are centrally concerned with values. The second premise on which managerial effectiveness rests is that to achieve effectiveness, the manager has particular knowledge and understanding, usually termed management expertise, which if applied will result in the organization achieving effectiveness. In other words, the manager is maintaining that there is a branch of knowledge which claims that social organizations are predictable in their behaviour and susceptible to considerable manipulation given a particular set of circumstances. What is clear, however, is that such knowledge does not exist. We have only to consider the attempts of social scientists, governments and economists to predict both human behaviour and outcomes to see that this is an enterprise fraught with uncertainty, not subject to iron laws. It is simply not possible to predict things such as levels of employment, inflation or interest rates with certainty – if it were, then the UK would not have been in the mess it has been. Not only is the knowledge that is claimed by managers a fiction, but organizations are made up of individuals who paradoxically have the need to render aspects of their lives predictable, while at the same time wanting to maintain freedom and individuality. Individuals, either wittingly or unwittingly, will find ways to circumvent bureaucracy and resist the regime of checking, surveillance and accountability endemic within managerialism. The conflict between us and them, the manager and the managed, is greatly exacerbated by way of the inability of the manager to deliver effectiveness and efficiency. This is not, however, to dismiss the harm and damage often committed in the vain attempts to succeed, but as McIntyre observes, 'Our social order is in a literal sense out of our and indeed anyone's control. No one is or could be in charge' (McIntyre 1985).

Despite the 'moral fiction' of the manager, managerialism shows a grim determination to survive. Some of those who forged their reputations with management primers in the 1970s and 1980s have begun to recognize the precariousness of their positions. Time and experience have demonstrated the fallibility of their expertise, exposing it to be what McIntyre refers to as 'expressions of arbitrary, but disguised will and preference' (McIntyre 1985). However, survival is the thing, so the manager who previously claimed expertise which was rooted in his or her ability to render human activity as predictable, now claims it on the basis of his knowledge about how unpredictable human activity actually is. Who said leopards couldn't change their spots? So we find the experts abandoning the 'search for excellence' (Peters and Waterman 1982) and claiming we must 'thrive on chaos' (Peters 1989). As managerialism attempts to hang on to the coat tails of moral theory, the 'new' managerial insights are presented as 'paradoxical' (Handy 1994) or 'revolutionary'. Abandoning the earlier incantation, Tom Peters now urges managers to embrace the management revolution. 'It challenges what we thought about managing ... Most fundamentally the times demand that flexibility and love of change replace our long-standing penchant for mass production and mass markets based as it is upon a relatively predictable environment now vanished' (Peters 1989). We need hardly add, 'and which was never there'. What is now being proposed as the latest managerial exhortation is yet another fiction. If we are to celebrate and embrace unpredictability through creating what

Peters calls self-managing teams which are flexible, which special-
ize, are differentiated and are comfortable with change or innova-
tion, then this is not a successful organization, since the outcomes
might, by definition, be unpredictable. Again, as McIntyre notes,
'organisational success and organisational unpredictability exclude
one another' (McIntyre 1985).

However, whatever the reasons behind the change of heart there
is an important message here, in that there may well be a more
dynamic relationship between organizational success and organizational unpredictability. What Peters (1989) is arguing for is a very
significant conceptual leap, he is recognizing that change is by and
large uncontrollable. On the one hand everything is changing (nothing stays the same) but it is impossible to control the changes. This
may appear at first as a recipe for disaster – it isn't. To understand
and acknowledge this fact is profoundly important for a headteacher
as it releases the headteacher from the stress often induced by the
pressure to 'control' and allows energy to be expended in much
more fruitful ways. The question that Peters tries to come to terms
with in business is an important question that headteachers would
do well to ponder. If, as a headteacher, I am not in the business
of 'controlling' change, then what business am I in? Put simply, the
business is in creating a culture in which change is both constant
and challenging. It is the responsibility of headteachers to manage an
environment fraught with potential problems in a way which promotes
constant change as the norm. To achieve this means working with
and through people and also means to a large extent relinquishing
the notion that you can control what others are doing. It means
supporting, encouraging and arguing with people as they also seek
to improve and develop what they are doing. Because headteachers
are 'managing' schools, they must also accept the responsibility to
educate and equip others with the knowledge and skills required to
meet the challenges.

This particular view of management, namely the recognition that
efforts to control are essentially futile, has led to some exciting and
radically different workplaces because of the ways they are 'managed'. What is being offered is a new radical agenda for headteachers
which has two major headings. The first heading is what headteachers need to be like in terms of attitudes and qualities and the
second is what they need to do.

The first of these headings is very fundamental. The characteristics
of successful headteachers are often a list of behaviours or actions.
What lies behind the behaviours and actions will, however, be particular values and attitudes. Fullan (1993) writes about the 'new work

of principals', arguing that the changing nature of the work demands a change in the way headteachers think about the job and themselves. Fullan (1993), quoting Serge, suggests that the important attributes of the headteacher are those of a teacher, in that what is being organized is learning. As a headteacher, you are organizing and managing a learning process in which adults are learning new knowledge and skills and applying them in new situations. Running a school therefore has all the highs and lows of running a classroom.

Management as teaching is a powerful and exciting metaphor. It requires deep understanding of learning, it is imbued with great integrity – consider the nature of the pupil–teacher relationship – it seeks enlightenment and it seeks to empower and embolden those it touches. Management as teaching demands a high degree of flexibility, but it also needs a constant and recurring concern to develop and preserve human relationships.

The most successful teaching recognizes the importance of the interaction between teacher and children. The best teachers are constantly creating new ways in which they can encourage children to reflect upon what they know, use what they know in new situations and gradually come to 'make sense' of new ideas or concepts. Teachers maintain the fine balance between guiding and telling, they provoke reflection, challenge assumptions and illuminate ways to proceed. They lead by example, displaying tolerance, patience and kindness. They model their own expectations and continually inspire and stimulate. Teaching is educational leadership, critical, ethereal, transformative and educative.

In schools, as in classrooms, there is less need for hierarchy, but more need for groups and individuals focused upon specific tasks. They need systems and structures within which the main priority is to feed back new learning, rather than adopting a monolithic ethos or culture within which people are unable to learn in a variety of environments and situations. Many of these assertions will be developed further in later chapters, but it is perhaps worth bearing in mind the real possibilities for success. Arguably schools are among the best managed human organizations anywhere, since the people who manage them bring to bear the skills, knowledge, values and attitudes which enabled them to be successful teachers. In other words, they bring attitudes to the task of managing which are essential for successful organizations. There is a current argument that the best teachers should be encouraged to remain in the classroom and there is certainly some merit in making this more possible. However, perhaps a proportion of our 'best' teachers should also be encouraged to seek to become headteachers simply *because* they are our best teachers.

Old style management training paid scant regard to headteacher experience as teachers, but perhaps future training should focus much more upon those early successful teaching years as the key to good management.

Headteachers, or those charged with the responsibility of running our schools in effective and efficient ways, will identify with some of the dilemmas surrounding the revised wisdom of managerialism and the realities of a working life. No doubt headteachers will find particular resonance in the understanding of how unpredictable life in a school can be. The list of possible events, occurrences and circumstances merely emphasizes the profound impact of contingency upon school development. The promotion of a senior member of staff to another school, unforeseen illness, uncertainty about budget allocation, lack of precision about pupil numbers (and we could go on *ad nauseam*) all impact to a greater or lesser extent upon how schools operate. This list does not even touch upon the added human drama which is also a fundamental and significant characteristic of schooling, and which dictates much of the day-to-day life of working organizations. Given this, the only explanation for schools being subjected to the overwhelming exhortation to plan and document every aspect of school is the misguided assumption that writing something down guarantees that it will happen.

3

WHAT DOES IT MEAN

TO BE A

HEADTEACHER?

There are perhaps two certainties in education, neither of which is particularly comforting. The first is that education, and primary schools in particular, will continue to exist within a climate that demands more and more change. For those who may yearn for a past life of a settled nature when teachers could 'just get on with the job' the outlook is grim. The second certainty is that the nature of primary headship will become more complex, more demanding and much more difficult to pin down in terms of the exact requirements of the job. In some ways it is already impossible to address a group of primary headteachers as if they were a homogeneous group which shares an identical or similar set of concerns and problems. The fact is that the very nature of headship will largely depend upon the specific circumstances in which the role is being played out. The problems facing a headteacher in a small rural primary school will be very different from those in a large urban school. The local community will inevitably bring its own unique pressures to bear on the local schools, grant-maintained schools will have their own particular agendas and even now local education authorities may have widely differing expectations from their primary headteachers. So in one sense any attempt to define or even describe the nature of headship risks a range of generalizations (and possibly platitudes) which, while attempting to appeal to everyman, actually fail to touch the lives of anyone. It is this, then, that forms the basis of our challenge, and at this point we must be very clear that there are no easy, 'hand me down' solutions, or strategies which can be universally employed. To suggest any such thing would be to renege upon our earlier sentiment. Whatever else headship is, it is by necessity messy, imprecise and often uncertain.

If we reject the managerial, technicist view of headship, however, we are still left with the task of charting a course through the twisting and tortuous circumstances that contribute to most primary headteachers' daily lives. These circumstances are not made easier by the increasingly ambiguous and ambivalent position in which you find yourselves. It is a strange paradox that has been created by recent government policies on education. Primary headteachers are being encouraged to be much more assertive and autonomous in terms of their managerial role and to demonstrate an independence of mind and spirit. You are being urged to break out of the control of local education authorities, to embrace the market place and to seek to define the particular characteristics of your schools through developing centres of excellence, selecting a proportion of the intake and making decisions about spending priorities. At the same time, the government is exerting a centralized control of the major aspects of education, including the curriculum, assessment arrangements and relationships with governors and parents. What this means is that, while you are being urged to develop skills and strategies with which to manage your schools, the areas which are 'open' to being managed are increasingly prescribed. Managing a school is being regarded less and less as making decisions about real educational issues – that is, issues concerned with teaching and learning – and much more as efficiently and effectively achieving ends which have been imposed from outside. You, even as an entrepreneurial headteacher, will find yourself in an increasingly regulated and controlled system.

A further challenge for you as a primary headteacher in the late 1990s is that it is a peculiar feature of British life that education is still a central party political issue. While it is the case that in most Western democracies education is a political concern, in that any service which demands so much of the public purse is of legitimate interest, in Britain education is so bound up with class that it is argued about by groups which carry with them the particular values espoused by specific political parties. This inevitably leads to value conflicts within the life of schools, since most schools include within their parent body, teaching staff and governing body a variety of people who hold the range of political values which can crudely be formulated into educational values. Even if for one moment we could imagine that you as a primary headteacher did not have your own values, it is not difficult to appreciate the difficulty of being at the centre of such potentially polarized views about schooling. Trying to reconcile the perspectives of teachers, students, parents, governors and government can in itself put enormous strain upon headteachers. If nothing else, you need to be steadfast and resolute in maintaining your own position and integrity. So how can we find our way through this difficult terrain? One area which may provide some assistance is that branch of educational studies which has looked at the nature and purpose of educational leadership and the relationship or impact that leadership has upon the culture of a particular school.

The nature and purpose of school leadership is itself a contested area. There is an increasing body of literature which puts leadership alongside management suggesting that they are comfortable bedfellows. To the management theorist, leadership is seen as one aspect of management; indeed, leadership is defined in management terms and is regarded as part of the manager's armoury. It is a view of leadership which is comfortable in discussing 'leadership styles', and assumes that leadership is embodied in the office rather than the person, and that it is an intricate part of managerial hierarchy. It also has appeal to managers, since it is a managerial concept which is difficult to pin down, and therefore goes some way to satisfying the critics of managerialism who reject the scientific objectivity that managerialism claims. When managers talk about leadership, it reassures them that here finally could be a concept behind which they can hide, since it is one which is not amenable to scientific investigation. Hence new managerialists will bring forth new incantations to further mesmerize their audience. 'The Managers do things right: leaders do the right thing. The Manager administers; the leader ministers' (Bennis 1989). This view of leadership, however, is one that merely apes those values inherent within managerialism. Leadership is just another way to get people to do what the manager wants. It is leadership burdened with the values and attitudes which for many teachers and headteachers are inimical to the business of education. To offer this understanding of leadership is to suggest that the complex can be reduced to a series of managerial techniques, as Foster says: 'To see leadership as a managerial virtue is to see it as a powerless attempt to control and predict human action' (Foster 1989).

What we need, then, is a new idea of educational leadership which is appropriate for schools, which reflects democratic values and which can itself be defined within educational terms. In other words, because the nature of education is distinct from that of manufacturing or business organizations, so educational leadership should be distinct. It is not unreasonable to suggest that educational leadership should be educational and therefore should be defined in terms that have meaning within educational discourse. There are two distinct views of leadership which provide a starting point.

The first is referred to by Burns (1978) as transactional leadership. In many ways this describes the types of leadership discussed above. It is a leadership which is an exchange between the leader and the led, often underpinned by specific reference to goals and targets set by the leader and achieved by the led. In some sense this transition is negotiated. In schools, teachers can be rewarded for particular tasks, they can be cajoled, bullied, bribed or persuaded to do certain things. If the negotiations are successful between the headteacher and the teacher harmony can ensue, and a degree of progress is made. An example of transactional leadership may be a request by a headteacher to a member of staff to produce a particular policy document within a certain time. This may be rewarded by an extra point on the salary scale for the duration of the task. In all likelihood, the policy will be produced, readily available to staff, governors and inspectors, and the teacher will feel that the effort was worthwhile. The implication here is that transactional leadership can work at a particular level. It may improve the ability to achieve certain targets or goals, but essentially it is operating in a static environment, one that to most intents and purposes is unchanging. The policy has been produced, and there is a degree of satisfaction all round that the task is complete. This form of leadership is contrasted by Burns (1978) with what he refers to as transformative leadership. This view of leadership takes a radically different starting point. Rather than being grounded within action, as is transactional leadership, transformative leadership introduces an ethical basis to leadership, and implicit within it is a philosophical dimension. Transformative leadership is concerned with changing the way people think, along with changing the reality with which they work. It is the idea of transformation which brings to leadership an educational dimension. If we consider the earlier example, transformative leadership would not simply seek a new policy document but would, through the process of producing the document, wish critically to consider and evaluate the relevant curriculum area or aspect of schooling. Transformative leadership is like the transactional in that it is dependent upon a leader having followers, but there is the determination to offer others the opportunity to engage with and change the way they think about a particular issue. In this sense, teachers can be transformed through participation, involvement and critical reflection. Burns discusses transformative leadership in terms of values and morality.

'Leaders engage with followers, but from higher levels of morality; in the enmeshing of goals and values both teachers and followers are raised to more principled levels of judgement. Much of this kind of elevating leadership asks *from* followers rather than merely promising them goods' (Burns, quoted in Foster 1989). This ability of leadership to transform people, situations and organizations has provided a further impetus to managerialism to hijack the idea and use it to develop managerial techniques further. Any organization, schools included, finds it hard to resist the idea of the leader who inspires and transforms. Unfortunately, this only brings us back to where we started. Put in managerial terms, transformative leadership is just another way of manipulating people, but instead of offering increasing rewards, management ensures that the manipulated 'feel good' about their work. It is, to put it crudely, just another 'means to an end'.

It would be disingenuous not to acknowledge the positive impact on school life of transformational leadership. By its very nature it has meant that teachers have participated much more in decision-making, it has led to an increased awareness of the part of head-teachers of the importance of communication and it has forced management training to confront the issue of teacher involvement and empowerment and therefore recognized the central importance to successful schools of the quality of relationships. While acknowledging the positive impact that this has made upon management studies, it is necessary to develop further the notion of leadership within a moral and ethical framework rather than as a means to an end. To be of more practical use to headteachers, transformational leadership and its particular characteristics needs to be further explored. It is also important to consider the location of leadership as not solely residing in the position of headteacher.

To consider where leadership may occur, however, is to confront one of the paradoxes of the school improvement research (see, for example, Fullan 1991; Stoll and Fink 1996). While on the one hand the headteacher is identified as the defining feature of a successful school, to the extent that the quality of the headteacher is the single most important factor in the success or otherwise of the school, on the other hand we are also aware that for successful change to occur, teachers need to be empowered and genuinely involved in the process of change. To dismiss this paradox by simply arguing that good headteachers empower teachers misses the point about the importance of values. The question still needs to be posed: do head-teachers empower teachers because it gets the job done, or because there is an intrinsic value placed upon empowering teachers?

Transformative leadership is not necessarily invested with specific values, and emphasizes leadership residing in an individual. What follows from transformative leadership is that all those within the school will require some important knowledge of the whole school, and there will need to be sufficiently well structured arrangements to ensure that issues and concerns are subject to some degree at least of debate and argument. In many ways, transformative leadership is able to demonstrate a sound ethical base, as it begins to open up a more detailed definition of leadership.

The ethical basis for educational leadership is not a new idea. Grace (1995) demonstrates that much of English schooling has been centrally concerned with what it means to lead a good life. Education itself has been a powerful influence upon both the defining of a good life and the means of attaining one. What has happened is that the liberal culture which represented educational practice in ethical terms has been seriously damaged by the new managerialism. If the view of education as an ethical enterprise requires liberation from the current oppressors then other notions of leadership may prove fruitful. For those involved in critical leadership studies, it is entirely proper that ethical consideration should be of crucial import-ance in consideration of leadership. As Foster says,

> Leadership in general must maintain an ethical focus which is oriented towards democratic values within a community. This has to do with the meaning of ethics historically – as a search for the good life of a community ... Ethics here refers to a more comprehensive construct than just individual behaviour; rather it implicates us in how we as a moral community live our communal lives.
>
> (Foster 1989)

It is this deeply republican view of schooling, together with the belief in a moral community, which postulates leadership as a social func-tion rather than a particular general attribute. It is also a belief that educational values should be grounded within democratic ideals, which in turn should also inform the nature of leadership itself. It is, as Foster points out, 'crucial to understand that while leadership may occur in organisational settings and may be exercised by posi-tion holders, there is no necessary or logical link between the two concepts' (Foster 1989).

While it may not be 'lonely at the top', leaders do need followers. The notion that as a headteacher you can march purposefully off into a future without followers would merely transform you into an eccentric crank. The future, whatever it might look like, needs to be the subject of negotiation, it needs to command respect and commitment. Leadership can only be exercised within a social con-text. To view leadership through the values of politics, community and morality is to draw a very thick line between leadership and management, despite the determination of management to present it as a managerial technique.

> The lack of distinction between management and leadership has become such a common feature of our language that we are often hard pressed to recognise that leadership can be disorganised, little concerned with production, uncaring of feelings and still be effective if the power of ideas is commanding.
>
> (Foster 1989)

To consider leadership from this perspective, and in an effort to ground it in practice, Foster suggests that there are four particular attributes which leadership should embody. As well as being transformative, leadership should include critical, educative and ethical dimensions. In a sense, these attributes or characteristics of leadership are an extension of Schön's (1983) view of the reflective practitioner. Foster is offering a view of leadership in action which provides guidelines for reflection while simultaneously providing a view of successful leadership. At the root of this view of leadership is the notion of human agency. It implies fundamentally that human beings are not passive recipients of action, but that their world, or reality, is constructed by them and, more importantly, can be changed by them. Educational leadership celebrates the facility of a school to construct and achieve its own future through what Barber (1996) has referred to as 'restless evaluation'. At the heart of human agency is the entirely healthy, constantly critical appraisal of the status quo. Being critical implies the possibility of change through a degree of professional dissatisfaction. It implies looking at the present with an appreciation of the possibility for development and a willingness to bring new understandings to bear upon the present circumstances. To be uncritical is simply to manage the present, often in an unsatisfactory manner, which culminates in the dependency culture written about and described by Fullan (1992) as the 'if only . . .' syndrome. Schools which enjoy critical leadership, from headteachers and teachers, flourish, develop and preserve a sense of excitement and professional commitment to a fundamental educational value, a search for improvement through reflection. This implies particular practices and modes of behaviour which will be explored in later chapters, but suffice it to say that it has very significant implications for an approach to staff development and continuing teacher education. It would be understandable if at this point headteachers and teachers threw their hands up in collective despair. The overwhelming experience of the previous decade in education has been characterized by, first, teachers being extremely critical of the nature and pace of change, but, second, as a very consequence of this, not having the opportunity to reflect. The overload of reform and initiative has clearly militated against this view of leadership, but at the same time the cultural change within our schooling is making the need for critical reflection even more necessary. Being critical does not mean being constantly angry, irritated or frustrated, but does mean bringing different realities to bear upon a school's predicament and matching those against the present.

Following on from critical leadership is the notion that leadership should be transformative. We have already looked at some of the implications of this in contrast to transactional leadership, but it is worth dwelling further on the ways in which it is closely allied with the critical dimension of leadership. Transformative leadership, as Burns (1978) suggested, is concerned to transform, or change, the situation, but more importantly it is also concerned to alter the way people think. This is not, however, to seek change for the sake of change. In some respects this element of the leadership agenda is perhaps the most fundamental and leads into an aspect of schooling which is currently the subject of some debate, namely the nature of school culture. This subject will be looked at in more detail below but it may be important at this stage simply to note that any discussion about transformative leadership must have at its root the transformation of the school culture. As Fullan has written, the ultimate aim of educational change should be to develop an ability to manage change (Fullan 1991). It is the sense that transforming the way people think should focus their minds and energy not just on the way the school views specific aspects of schooling, but on the institution's overall ability to alter its reality. Transformative leadership is a very powerful force. Examples of such leaders would include individuals such as Ghandi or Martin Luther King, and would also include organizations such as Amnesty International and Greenpeace. In terms of schooling, transformative leadership will affect some of the larger issues concerned with the treatment of children, the ethos of care and concern and the school's relationships with various stakeholders. Transformative leadership is, in a very real sense, about winning hearts and minds through the power of ideas.

It would seem entirely appropriate that educational leadership should be defined as educative. The two previous dimensions, critical and transformative, are clearly part of an educative process in that they encourage a questioning, sceptical but optimistic view of school life. They are concerned to promote questions, thoughts and critical enquiry – all aspects of a good education. Leadership which is educative must therefore be committed to involving itself in organizational

structures which facilitate debate, discussion and response. This
implies a determination to communicate widely and to ensure that
forums are such that everyone involved is comfortable to voice an
opinion and that a range of views are acceptable. A further element
within Foster's view of educative leadership is the responsibility
to remain in touch with a past. In this way, educative leadership
develops a strong sense of continuity, and is concerned to build and
develop upon the past stories of individual schools. Educative leadership should offer, according to Foster, both vision and analysis, and
should assist in the reflective process.

The final aspect of leadership, the ethical dimension, also has distinct strands. Educative leadership must be ethical both in terms of
the way individuals treat each other, and in the determination to
create a school which is a moral community. If we explore the first
element then we immediately return to the, by now, familiar territory
of leadership and management, or the managerial view of leadership. If leadership is to be ethical then essentially it must have a
determination not to treat people as simply means to an end. There
is a fundamental distinction between leadership and the wielding
of power. Foster is very clear: 'Treating people as means is to de-
humanise them, yet this is often the result of "leadership" training
programmes which see the task as the end and person as the means
to accomplish that end' (Foster 1989). This touches the very core
of an individual leader's behaviour, whether as headteacher, senior
management or curriculum coordinator. Perhaps this harsh distinction between means and ends is unrealistic, and Foster's idealism
fails to emphasize the need actually to get something done. This is
to suppose, of course, that the two things are mutually exclusive, but
if critical leadership studies have anything to offer then they must
be able to demonstrate that the commitment to work with people
ethically is also the way to achieve results. The second element within
ethical leadership is the development of a moral community as distinct from a collection of individuals. Educative leadership must be
concerned to confront the democratic formation of communities
which have at their heart values which reflect the community, rather
than the individual. The debate about the relationship between
individuals and their communities is very current and touches upon
deeply held beliefs, but educational leadership, if it is to be ethical,
must be concerned with the search for the good life of a community within the Aristotelian tradition. Outside schools, the sense of
community is being eroded, as is demonstrated by the incidence
of politicians' laments about the loss of community values. Edward
Luttwark (1994) writes: 'It is mildly amusing that nowadays the

standard Republican/Tory after dinner speech is a two-part affair, in which part one celebrates the virtues of unimpeded competition and dynamic structural change, while part two mourns the decline of the family and community "values" that were eroded precisely by the forces commended in part one.' Within schools, however, we need a genuine commitment to continue the quest.

Foster's ideas are radical and challenging. They confront educational leadership with some of the values of education itself and form an alternative agenda to that usually presented through management courses. They emphasize the process operating in school organizations and provide a perspective upon the potential relationships which could exist between headteachers and other members of staff. This does, however, relegate ends to a position which may appear to be negligible or even irrelevant. In other words, a straightforward reading of Foster emphasizes processes of educational leadership without paying much regard to tangible ends. This can lead us into difficult territory. On the one hand we can emphasize the process as both the means and the ends, since the means embody the values which can also be identified as ends. For example, if an educational aim (or end) is to promote the values inherent within democracy, then these values must permeate the organization of schooling.

This would imply that as long as ends and means are compatible, or indeed the same, then a way forward can be discerned. However, not all educational aims can be defined simply in terms of values. The primary curriculum, as well as being concerned with values, is also concerned with knowledge and skills. Primary school headteachers do not need reminding that educational ends also include the acquisition of the basic skills of literacy and numeracy, and they are under significant pressure to ensure that all pupils succeed in these areas. To state this allows us to confront some of the real dilemmas facing primary headteachers. School leadership cannot be defined solely in terms of the relationships and structures which relate only to adults. School leadership must also be defined in terms of the relationships, structures and opportunities which children experience, and these elements are not always compatible. Headteachers may find themselves in the position of arbitrating between the organizational processes and the educative, classroom processes. We can illustrate this by example. A school, by whatever means, has identified some serious weaknesses in its approach to the teaching of reading. Not surprisingly, it embarks upon a thorough review of current practice with a view to setting in place new procedures and approaches to teaching reading. An adherence to democratic values would mean that there was full collective discussion among all staff (and perhaps parents) before new procedures could be put into place. However, this may take a significant amount of time: getting all staff together is time consuming and often progress can be slow, especially if agreement is elusive. In the meantime children are not being taught to read successfully. How long, therefore, should this situation continue, how long should discussion continue in the interests of democracy, given that children's reading is suffering? The key element here is accountability and how that works within a structure which takes into account the hierarchy of school and classrooms. We come up again, however, against the managerial notion of accountability through being 'responsible to or for' rather than some moral rendering of accountability within a moral community or indeed a moral institution. Accountability within the moral community is not rooted in performance indicators or appraisal interviews, but within a framework of self-governing institutions in which all members, teachers and pupils are free to be themselves and where their accountability is rendered meaningful through the agreed and shared purposes of the school. Individual accountability shares the same ground as the accountability of the school. In a genuinely republican school the individual members of the school community are entirely comfortable with the aims and purposes of the institution. What this means, continuing the above example, is that all staff would share the sense of urgency to give their collective commitment to equip children with such a basic skill as reading. In this sense they are accountable to children and parents.

While much of this will appear as idealistic and other-worldly, given the current climate of operation, it nevertheless begins to impress primary headteachers with what they are confronted with. Discussions about the nature of leadership are important but they lead to a wider conclusion than that which can be encompassed within a particular style or version of leadership. In the final analysis, what we are clawing our way towards is the creation of a climate, a tone or a particular school culture which manifests the values and principles of the school. Once again, however, there are difficulties. First, managerialism also has some claims on being aware of the importance of the nature of organizational culture. As the proponents of managerialism are confronted by the limitations of their incantations they seek new avenues to explore. Culture is seen as such a new avenue. Organizational culture is, ironically, a feature of organizations which may have been instrumental in exposing the limitations of managerialism. The story could be told about how the theories of managerialism were entirely correct, but the culture of the organization prevented the ideas from taking hold: in effect people were not ready for the initiatives, there was no cultural tradition which embraced new ideas. Perhaps another version of the story is to equate cultural tradition with people's bloody minded-ness and an entirely reasonable scepticism about the expectations of management on the part of teachers or any other workers. It is a claim that is made with particular reference to primary education. The Chief Inspector's frustrations about the apparent unwillingness of teachers to engage in a debate about teaching strategies was attrib-uted to the particular culture of the primary school (Woodhead 1995). What we are again presented with is the desire to manipulate the culture to achieve particular ends and, for some, these ends would not be desirable. In industrial terms, and increasingly in educational terms, people are being asked to collaborate in their own demise, and it is hardly surprising that there may be some resistance to, or cynicism about, new working patterns which are aimed at creating a different culture.

The second difficulty is concerned with the concept of culture. The culture of an organization is very difficult to pin down or to get to grips with. An indication of the level of difficulty is the number of definitions of what the culture of the school might actually mean. Hargreaves and Hopkins (1991) define it as 'the procedures, values and expectations that guide people's behaviour within an organisa-tion', which echoes the simpler definition of Deal (1987) as 'the way we do things around here'. Jennifer Nias (1989), in her work on the lives of teachers, talks about 'the beliefs and values of a group' as lying at the heart of its culture. Within the variety of definitions, it is important to emphasize the central notion of values as an embodiment of a school culture. A school culture can manifest itself in a variety of ways, but fundamentally it is based on its values and beliefs. The way the school operates is an expression of its own individual culture – its own individual set of values and beliefs. Since a school's culture is an expression of belief and attitudes as assumed and acted upon by the teachers working in the school, the culture of each school is unique. While schools have their own particular culture, that culture is not a static entity. Culture is con-stantly changing, values and beliefs are often argued over and in a sense this is what provides schools with opportunities. The point to grasp as a headteacher is that the culture of schools can change, that culture is open to influence, argument, demonstration and therefore re-creation. It can be argued that the real job of school leadership is to create and sustain a school culture which does embody and celebrate those values and beliefs which operate within the moral community and which rejects the scientific managerialism of ends justifying means.

Although school cultures can change, and it is not difficult to imagine ways in which things are 'done around here' as being subject to review, they also provide a sense of continuity in the life of a school. As we have noted earlier, a key element in leadership is an understanding of a school's past and an appreciation about how it has arrived at its present state. In this sense, a school's culture is also defined by traditions and the stories that are told about the events and characters which have shaped its development. So although culture is amenable to change, it is also important to remember that a school's culture provides a large measure of stability and indeed predictability about the way things are done. This is something of a paradox, inasmuch as a school's tradition provides a touchstone and a sense of security, but it may also be the very aspect of the school which is working against moving a school forward. So how do cultures change? Most school cultures are in a constant state of flux through the arrival of new teachers, through the altering views and practices of existing teachers and with the perpetual turnover of children. All these, of course, are aspects of everyday life in many primary schools. They are not static institutions in which ideas or feelings are fixed. We can refer to this as cultural evolution.

School culture can, however, be altered radically and in some cases rapidly. In an earlier chapter we discussed the nature of the national debate about education being seen as a cultural battle. The New Right is making a concerted and determined effort to alter the way the public, teachers and headteachers think about education and how it is structured. This has been achieved through a variety of means, including regulations which have fundamentally altered the structure and administration of education. Evidence of the cultural change can be seen not only in the public arena of accountability, the emphasis upon surveillance and an undermining of LEAs, but also in the minutiae of school life. Small-scale cultural change can be demonstrated in minutes of governors' meetings, the list of in-service courses and the diminishing list of extra-curricular activities. What has happened in the past eight years has been an attempt at a cultural revolution in education which has undoubtedly had some significant impact, but that is not to say that it has been successful.

In a school setting there is the possibility of radical and rapid change. Some people or events make a sufficient impact upon cultural boundaries to change the way things are done quickly, but the question remains: have they changed the way people think? Have they altered the attitudes and feelings of teaching staff? Have they forced teachers to rethink their own values? These are difficult questions and there are no easy answers. Responses would vary. For some teachers the arrival of a new headteacher might affect the way they think and talk about their work, it may lead to a reassessment of their practice or views about children's learning. For others, it could simply mean a reaffirmation of their own prejudices, and a confirmation that changing things never helped, and in this sense may lead to entrenchment and resentment. It would seem that any discussion about school cultures assumes that there is a desirable culture which it is worthwhile to create and maintain, and it is important to examine that notion more closely.

If we are to try to discuss what a desirable culture may be like, we need to remind ourselves about what kind of values we are propounding. To view culture and structure as interdependent, as is the view put forward by Stoll and Fink (1996), is to assume that structure equates with behaviour. Culture can be almost entirely divorced from structure, but not from values and ultimately not from behaviour. Indeed, Stoll and Fink concede that structures can be changed without seriously affecting culture, so it is difficult to sustain an argument upholding their interdependency. For instance, as part of their structure, most schools have staff meetings or senior staff meetings. These are not in themselves particularly indicative of a school's culture. The way people behave within those meetings, what is acceptable or unacceptable, the allocation and location of powers, and the attitude to conflict and disagreement would be much better indicators of what the culture of the school is like. To begin really to describe a desirable culture we need to look at fundamental values and how they may be manifested; this may have some implications for structures, but would have much more fundamental implications for the nature and quality of the relationships within the school.

If we briefly revisit the earlier discussion on leadership, it may begin to point towards some indicators of what a desirable school culture should include. There are several elements or even requirements needed to sustain the view of leadership propounded earlier, especially if we are to maintain that leadership should be based within a community rather than residing with one person and if it is to be critical, transformative, educative and ethical. If leadership is to be critical, then there are clear implications for the nature of school culture. If those in school are to be critical, they need an understanding of the processes or enterprises with which they are concerned. In terms of education and schooling, this goes beyond knowledge of teaching and learning to an appreciation of a wider view of education. This understanding needs to be guided by what it means to be educated as a citizen within a democracy rather than by technological or industrial utilitarianism. Those who work in a school should have, as part of their agenda, an engagement with the notion of education in its widest sense, and this includes its philosophy and sociology. In short, teachers need a politics on which to ground their activities and to fit their own learning and understanding. It is reflection upon the past which should inform the future, which also implies that teachers need knowledge of a past. In effect, all schools need a sense of their own story and how it fits with the narratives of others.

If we simply expect schools to have a view of their own possibilities which are somehow disconnected from a politics then we are failing to sustain an awareness of what the real meaning and purpose of education is about. If schools are to be successful, they must be critical; if they are to be critical they must engage with the social context within which they are operating and by which they are sustained. What we are saying here is that part of the desirable culture within schools should be a willingness and determination to engage in debate about the very nature of education itself and its role in society. In a sense the school, to borrow Schön's phrase, should be a reflective institution but not an introspective one.

Given that there is an awareness of the wider issues, the next element within the desirable culture is some common agreement about the actual part a particular school is to play in the life of those involved. Many writers will refer to a school's vision or mission statement and there are similarities here to that idea, but with a significant difference in emphasis. Simply to write about a school's vision or mission statement is to see schools as individual institutions without reference to the circumstances in which they are working. If, however, we arrive at common and shared agreements about the part this or that particular school is going to play in people's lives then that acknowledges that the school will be only one element through which people relate to other institutions, organizations or social groups. It is a view of the school as part of a community rather than separate from it. This view of schools also has implications about the range of people that schools may touch and in what ways. The desirable school culture will clearly have agreed assumptions about what part it might play in children's lives, and these assumptions will encompass achievement, learning, socializing, support and care. It will incorporate understanding about what part the school plays in the life of the staff, in terms of their achievements, training and so on. It will also have some regard to the part to be played in the life of the local community and the involvement of parents, governors and other groups. The possibility for a school to be a focus for community enrichment and invigoration has been demonstrated by schools up and down the land. It is a natural extension of the critical awareness of the nature of society for a school to have a clear view about the role it is to play in the life of its local community.

The last element in the desirable culture should concern itself with the ways in which people relate to each other. This has been signalled earlier in terms of the importance of people's behaviour but in some respects behaviour is the surface manifestation of a school's culture and we need to scratch the surface of that behaviour to try to identify the culture which it illustrates. In terms of behaviour and relationships, the school improvement research (Fullan 1991; Hargreaves and Hopkins 1991; Stoll and Fink 1996) has plenty to offer. The most productive relationships appear to be those which offer genuine collaboration between teachers, rather than a forced collegiality. This means teachers working together because they want to and deriving real benefits from planning together, observing each other and assisting each other in reflection about their work. Within this kind of working atmosphere there is support for initiatives and teachers feel able to take risks and make mistakes without fear of ridicule or criticism. This sounds rather cosy and it may well be, but it is not easy to achieve. There are other aspects to this culture which need to be borne in mind. The way in which dissent or disagreement is dealt with and the preparedness to live in uncomfortable times are crucial elements. It is very easy for everyone to agree about things which are unimportant, but this can mask fundamental disagreements which, if brought to the surface, could put the cosy atmosphere at risk. There are some important points to be made about disagreements or conflicts. The first point is that conflict is inevitable. Nothing will change or develop without a degree of conflict, but the critical test for you as a headteacher is how you deal with it. To see conflict as a setback, or worse a failure, is to misunderstand the processes at work. Because the primary classroom is characterized largely by harmonious relationships and the ethos of care, it is tempting to characterize primary school staffrooms in a similar vein. To emphasize harmony and consensus is not the sign of a healthy culture, it is more often the sign of an inability to cope with an acknowledged difference. As a headteacher, you will need to demonstrate the positive nature of disagreement. You must recognize problems as crucial starting points, as they are often occasions when the most productive learning takes place. You will need to remain focused upon the problem and the search for solutions without being side-tracked into personalized bickering. Fullan (1993) refers to problems as friends and argues that you cannot learn or be successful without them. To ignore or side-step problems will mean that change is superficial and trivial. This can mean some uncomfortable rides, especially for you as the headteacher, but bear in mind, the more uncomfortable the ride, the greater the satisfaction when the creative situation emerges.

There is another worthwhile point to make about difference of view or approach. The current orthodoxy of primary school management is to emphasize the idea of a whole-school approach to the extent that schools are required to produce a range of whole-school policies or guidelines covering all aspects of their curriculum and administration. This emphasis upon whole school can, if taken too far, lead to dull conformity. As a headteacher, you should welcome and encourage difference. The idea that a school culture should somehow become a monolithic ethos which dictates all aspects of activity will stifle creativity. It also works against some of those earlier aspects of leadership which encouraged primary headteachers to model critical enquiry. Schools, like other organizations, need to be multicultural. Pairs, groups and teams of teachers should be encouraged to develop their own cultures, they should not feel constrained or restricted by the dead hand of the whole-school policy, but should feel able to work in a variety of ways. Again, the greater the range of experience the greater the range of possible solutions. As a headteacher you will, of course, need to balance the idea of children's entitlement with the celebration of difference.

In most respects, to describe relationships between teachers is to also describe the desirable relationship between teachers and children, in the sense that that relationship also needs an ethical basis and a commitment to mutual respect. All relationships, between teachers themselves, teachers and children and among the children, need some understanding about the location of power and how that relates to responsibilities, the exercise of rights and accountability. In some cases there will be an element of coercion in all these aspects of relationships, if only because occasionally people must be forced to be free, but we will return to this at a later stage.

These three elements – the shared understanding about the nature of education, the part that particular schools will play in the life of their members and the nature of relationships – provide a broad outline of what headteachers need to begin to explore in order to develop a school culture that is ethically based, focused upon learning and dynamics. The discussion about school culture started with the suggestion that the creation and maintenance of such a culture is the most important job of leadership, and in that sense is the responsibility of all those in leadership positions. There is very little doubt that it is upon the headteacher that most responsibility will fall.

In the course of this chapter we have explored what it might mean to be a headteacher. We have looked at the nature of leadership and in particular suggested that leadership is a social construction, since leaders need someone to lead. We have also explored the notion of culture as a crucial dimension of leadership. There is a dilemma in any consideration of headship. On the one hand the idea of a leader does not sit comfortably in many primary schools, where the delegation of responsibility is perceived as important, but on the other hand there is an expectation that the headteacher will function as the leader. This chapter has endeavoured to explore what leadership could be like and to articulate the characteristics of successful leadership. Perhaps before drawing this chapter to a close, it is important to take a slightly different perspective and look at what might be the character of the leader. If headteachers are such important figures then what it means to be a headteacher implies an emphasis upon identity as much as character.

Recent work by Southworth (1995) has highlighted the general lack of investigation into the notion that being a headteacher is an 'occupational identity' rather than simply a job to be done. In his case study, the theory he proposes is that being a headteacher is closely allied to a very strong idea of self and that as people develop as headteachers they are essentially developing as people. In our own work with many headteachers there is much to suggest that when the subject of Southworth's case study talks about being a headteacher he is echoing the thoughts of many.

> It's [headship] extremely demanding, totally consuming of the person . . . it's time consuming . . . it's a way of life . . . It looks like someone really not doing anything other than things pertaining to headship. It's a hobby, everything. You get up in the morning and go to work and you think about it all day and you come home, perhaps, for supper, and you're still thinking about it and you go back and spend the whole evening there and you come back and you're still thinking about it. You try and shed it a little bit before you go to bed and then you get up and start the whole day again and that goes on and you just don't shed it, not ever.
>
> (Southworth 1995)

To repeat Southworth's observation, 'Headship was not a job, it was a way of life.' If this is the case, then we are confronted with a dimension to headship which has major implications. To some extent it puts into perspective our discussions about leadership and culture and brings them out of the social domain and into the realms of individual agency. Essentially, you may become a headteacher, but headteachering becomes you. It is the view that headteachers see themselves in a profession which encourages them to act out their own deepest beliefs, which in turn mediates their actions. If this is so, and Southworth's case is a good one, then rather than emphasize the characteristics of effective leadership we need to look much more at the character of leaders.

It would also suggest that as a headteacher you have to be very aware of your own personal resources and attributes. If Southworth is right, then self-knowledge becomes an important element in both preparing for and being a headteacher. It puts the personal firmly into the realm of professional. How you as the headteacher react and respond will be very important for everyone working in the school. As the headteacher, what you do and what you say will be scrutinized and analysed, since it is your reactions which are often the focus of attention. What you may regard as a flippant exchange, what for you was an off the cuff remark, can be taken very seriously by the receiver. Because of this you will need a sharp awareness of the perception of others. Whether you like it or not, others may regard the person who holds the position of headteacher with some awe.

As well as understanding other people's perceptions, it is important that you know and understand how you are liable to react in any given circumstances, and it is in this sense that self-awareness is important. Headteachers need to develop a range of attributes which will assist in creating the kind of relationships and culture we have discussed. For some these attributes come easily, for others they will be harder to acquire, but it is important that some modes of behaviour become habitual. Such behaviour might include:

◆ the ability to remain calm;
◆ a willingness to listen;
◆ a willingness to engage in debate;
◆ a preparedness to share and devolve power;
◆ a high degree of professional humility;
◆ the ability to make and maintain professional friendships;
◆ the ability to focus on problems not the person.

Being a headteacher, then, is both intensely personal and increasingly public.

What we can confirm is that running a school is fundamentally concerned with values and beliefs and, while structures and systems have a part to play in school organization, they only represent values and beliefs, and, further, that the way people behave within those structures is a very basic manifestation of the nature of the school culture. What is also clearly important is that headteachers play a crucial role in setting the tone and it is their own beliefs and values which will influence and dictate their actions, although influencing, creating and maintaining school culture is of course a two-way process. Given the powerful position of the primary headteacher, however, we can begin to explore how you can begin to work within the constraints and realities of everyday school life.

4

THE RHETORIC OF
SCHOOL DEVELOPMENT
PLANNING

A significant symbol of the promotion of a management culture in schools is the school development plan (SDP), the educational equivalent of the 'business plan'. The rapid growth of the SDP has resulted in a wealth of literature, guidance and courses, which embrace a planning orthodoxy that spans audit, review, evaluation and so on. We seem to have about reached a stage where every aspect of school life must be endorsed in an action plan, as if, as we have said above, writing something down means that it is going to happen.

The status assumed by the school development plan illustrates yet another paradox: while schools are being urged to engage in self-evaluation in order to identify and prioritize areas for improvement, at the same time a very clear agenda is being imposed from the centre which identifies improved standards and efficiency as being the goals to be achieved.

We would not argue that schools have no need to plan: quite the reverse. The pace of educational change over the past ten years has meant that if schools did not plan before, they have to do so now simply because of the wealth of tasks confronting them. In considering the fundamental purpose of school development planning it is worth retracing the steps which led it to the position it now occupies in management orthodoxy and to remind ourselves of the original intention of the SDP.

The rapid expansion of school development planning as a key management task resulted from attempts by schools to respond to the demands of a variety of groups and educational legislation. It is now generally overlooked that there is no statutory requirement, and nor has there ever been, for schools to have a school development plan, but there is an expectation that all will and an assumption that a well documented SDP should be available to any party with a legitimate interest in the management of the school. No head-teacher will be appointed unless he or she is able to talk about the purposes of school development planning and it is a major compon-ent of the new headteacher national qualification. In considering the purpose of development planning, it is worth tracing the history of its rise as an important aspect of school management, since its original purposes have been overlooked, or at least superseded, as it has assumed perhaps unwarranted status as a feature of an effect-ive school.

The notion of the school development plan had its origins in the 1970s. There were two issues at this time which highlighted an apparent need for more careful planning: the *ad hoc* nature of staff development and a lack of curriculum entitlement. Education had a high profile at this time, initiated to some extent by the James Report into teacher training needs (DES 1972), which emphasized the importance of in-service education to improve the quality of teaching. Subsequent reports by the ACSTT/INIST (1976, 1978) made recommendations about the need to make in-service education more school focused and the importance of a planned staff development programme. The second report also raised questions about a struc-ture within schools to establish their priorities for development.

Within this period and into the 1980s other national and local initiatives began to establish the need for forward planning. A survey of LEA curriculum policies published in 1979 by the DES revealed wide variations in practices among LEAs in terms of the existence and contents of curriculum guidance available to schools. The prim-ary survey by HMI (1978) identified a similar picture among schools themselves, citing inconsistencies in the breadth and balance of the curriculum offered in individual schools. The HMI Primary Survey called for improvements in curriculum development and manage-ment in the classroom and at whole-school level. Publication of *The School Curriculum* (DES 1981) echoed the call for a clearer structure to curriculum planning. It made reference to the need for LEAs to publish a curriculum statement and then for LEAs in their turn to require schools to develop whole-school policies on the curriculum. In addition, there was a perceived need for schools to formulate a more systematic approach to planning.

The strategy adopted by several LEAs is exemplified by the Inner London Education Authority's (ILEA's) publication *Keeping the School under Review* (1982). This document, and many similar publications by local education authorities around the country, was intended to assist schools with reviewing their effectiveness in a variety of areas. Inevitably the external imposition by LEAs of a framework for self-review was resisted in many schools. The areas identified for review did not always take account of a school's context and, while the basis of the publication was to enable schools to conduct an internal audit, certainly in the ILEA this was coupled with the intention to make schools more accountable. It also gave rise to a situation where answering a question almost became an end in itself, in that no action needed to result from the response. In the late 1970s and early 1980s, forty-one LEAs published similar 'school review' documents which they required schools to complete. A situation developed where schools were being asked questions as LEAs felt under pressure to make their schools accountable, but few reviews or responses elicited had a focus on quality.

This form of initiative, together with publications by HMI (1978) and the DES (1979, 1981), marked the beginning of calls from both national and local government for a better framework for forward planning for schools and a more coordinated approach to the provision of in-service education. The publication of *Better Schools* (DES 1985) emphasized the need for whole-school policies, together with regular review and assessment. The same publication also called for whole-school development to be supported by appropriate arrangements for staff development, which in turn laid the foundation for significant changes in funding arrangements for in-service training.

In view of the route subsequently taken in school development planning, it is ironic that the origin of the SDP can be traced to a move by the ILEA to raise the achievement of pupils. The ILEA secondary review, chaired by David Hargreaves, recommended an approach to school development in which individual schools identified areas for improvement. The primary review group led by ex-Chief HMI Norman Thomas published *Improving Primary Schools* (ILEA 1985), which had as its focus the need to enhance the confidence and achievement of children, particularly those from working-class backgrounds. The successful use of forward planning by individual schools to target improvements led to a formal recommendation in the report:

> We recommend that every school should have a plan for development, taking account of the policies of the Authority, the needs of the children, the capabilities of the staff and the known views of the parents. The plan should have an action sheet attached to it, showing what the responsibilities of members of staff will be and setting target dates ... The central purpose

should be expressed in terms of the improvements sought in the children's learning.

This local authority recommendation was endorsed at a national level a year later, when a report from the House of Commons Education, Science and Arts Select Committee recommended that

> every primary school should be required to operate according to a development plan agreed between it and the governing body or LEA . . . The plan should have an action sheet attached to it showing what the responsibilities of members of staff will be and setting target dates. A plan might well take more than a year and would be part of a continuing series . . . The central purpose should be expressed in terms of the improvements sought in children's learning.
>
> (House of Commons Education,
> Science and Arts Committee 1986)

Given that Norman Thomas acted as an advisor to the House of Commons Select Committee, the similarity in wording in the two recommendations is not surprising. Both the ILEA and the House of Commons reports also identified in-service training (INSET) as a powerful means of raising achievement, provided that the INSET was school-based rather than teachers attending external courses. A change of emphasis in INSET was recommended by the ILEA report:

> in-service training should move towards developing schools rather than individual teachers, with the bulk of in-service education for teachers being conducted at school level and, wherever it is conducted, being aimed at whole school improvement . . . the benefit to the individual teacher is important but secondary.
>
> (ILEA 1985)

Pressure for schools to undertake development planning was implicit in both the 1987 and 1988 Education Acts. The 1987 Education Act identified the duties and responsibilities of headteachers for the first time, many of which reflected the main tasks undertaken by headteachers over the previous thirty years. These included the general discipline and welfare of pupils, the management and organization of the school and effective use of all its resources, and establishing and maintaining good relationships within the school as well as with parents, governors and the LEA. A specific responsibility for the curriculum reflected the drive for a national framework with the requirement to develop a curriculum 'within the context of the National Curriculum'. There were two specific elements, however, within the prescribed responsibilities which related to development planning. Headteachers were required to define the aims and objectives of the school, to monitor and appraise the progress of the school and its staff and to manage appropriate staff development.

The massive implications of the 1988 Education Reform Act also highlighted the need for schools to engage in systematic forward planning. The introduction of the National Curriculum and statutory arrangements for assessment, and the devolution of funding through LMS, with the accompanying responsibilities for all aspects of resource budgeting and management, were to place significant demands on all schools. Schools, and headteachers in particular, were encouraged to view the formulation of a development plan as a means of demonstrating how new initiatives were to be accommodated and a plethora of statutory requirements met. The creation of a plan would demonstrate a strategy for systematic review and development of all aspects of management and enable schools to find a way through initiative overload.

It was at this point that the original purpose of development planning as envisaged by *Improving Primary Schools* (ILEA 1985), which was to focus the plan on the improvements sought in children's learning, began to be lost. Creating a plan became an end in itself, the expectation was that every school would have one and implicit in this expectation was the message that the quality of a development plan would act as an important indicator of the school's effectiveness. There was no shortage of advice and encouragement to schools and especially to headteachers. LEAs issued guidance, some required schools to submit their plans to the authority and the DES commissioned a research project to provide guidance at a national level. Schools invested considerable time and energy in devising their development plans. While undoubtedly the planning encouraged governors, headteachers and staff to develop a joint sense of direction and to engage in systematic planning in the long and short term, the appeal of the SDP was often that it would act as a security blanket. The production of a plan would enable a school to answer questions about all aspects of its work – and plans often addressed every element of school life, from building maintenance to developing community links. A development plan provided the opportunity to create an order of priority and activity for governors and staff. Inevitably this often related to budgeting, resources and the need to produce documentation for nine National Curriculum subjects, religious education and assessment.

Schools were encouraged to ensure that their plans incorporated development for the next three to four years, presumably as a result of the identification of this type of timescale at local authority level. 'We assume that most plans would take more than a year but less than four years to complete' (ILEA 1985). An inevitable result of formulating a detailed plan which covered all aspects of school life over a lengthy period was that much time and energy were invested in producing the plan itself, and many plans assumed encyclopaedic proportions. Apart from the ambitious nature of these sorts of plans, difficulties were created by an inability to take account of the inevitable changes which impact on all schools. Staff changes, absence, unforeseen budget cuts and so on are bound to occur within a three-to four-year period, resulting in a need to review, revise or perhaps abolish some aspects of forward planning. Ignoring the factors which impinge on many aspects of school management allowed those offering advice on development planning to develop guidance which was often unrealistic, particularly in the context of a primary school of even an average size.

The School Development Plan Project coordinated by David Hargreaves and David Hopkins is a good example of such guidance, which in this instance was sent to every school. Planning for School Development (Hargreaves *et al.* 1989) included detailed advice on audit and on negotiating and devising a plan, a process which the authors refer to as 'constructing and agreeing'. Much of the advice is sound, but ignores the fact that this was new territory for many schools. As a result this part of the process became an all-consuming task. Hargreaves *et al.* identified twelve possible areas for audit:

- pupils' diversity and achievements;
- curriculum provision and access;
- assessment and recording;
- teaching styles and methods;
- responsibilities of teaching staff;
- school management and organization;
- relationships with parents;
- partnerships with the local community;
- links with other schools and colleges;
- school, LEA and national documents;
- resources.

The recommendation is that any one of these might be the focus of an intensive audit each year, but that curriculum provision and resources require an annual audit. Again there is systematic advice on conducting a curriculum audit, but this identifies *what* needs to be done rather than suggesting *how* it could be done. The process suggested makes interesting reading, as it includes elements such as

- check whether the planned curriculum meets statutory requirements;
- identify possible gaps or overlap between subject areas;
- analyse the curriculum for each year group in terms of curricular objectives within and outside the National Curriculum;
- assess how much teaching time is available and how best to use it;
- compare *planned* provision with actual provision.

With the advantage of hindsight, can we really maintain that this was realistic advice given that, some years on, headteachers and subject coordinators are still concerned to find methods to monitor curriculum provision?

Again the advice on construction of the plan has some useful elements. The authors, for example, cite the fact that the plan should be realistic: 'neither too ambitious nor insufficiently demanding'. It is suggested that there should be no more than three or four major priorities: 'if the plan is realistic, it is more likely to be implemented.' There is a paradox in this type of advice set against the background of the very detailed procedures suggested for identifying priorities and the process outlined for formulating the plan with the involvement of governors and staff. The suggestion of twelve possible areas for inclusion in the plan and the need to set the plan in the context of the school's aims, national and local policies and initiatives, the school's own initiatives and any issues arising from the audit and consideration of available finance does militate against producing a plan which is 'short, sharp and focused'.

The difficulties of implementing a plan are acknowledged in all the literature about school development planning, including ironically the work by Hargreaves *et al.*: 'experience suggests that implementation does not proceed on automatic pilot' and 'the enthusiasm of even the most committed staff can flag when routine work and unanticipated events distract teachers from the tasks and targets' (Hargreaves *et al.* 1989). The remedy for this, it is suggested, lies with senior staff's own motivation and their ability to sustain commitment among their colleagues. Nowhere is it acknowledged that it might be the senior staff who are flagging as a result of having produced a plan which is over-ambitious or acting as a straitjacket rather than a guide.

There are two aspects of the guidance which are worthy of note. The first is that there is an assumption that there will be a large number of personnel available to share the workload in terms of audit and implementation. The frequent mention of senior staff, working parties or teams reflects a staffing structure which may well be unrealistic in many primary schools. Nowhere does the guidance mention the need to take this aspect into account when considering the context of the school. The second notable element is that the guidance is somewhat removed from the concept originally outlined in *Improving Primary Schools* (ILEA 1985) and the recommendation a year later by the House of Commons Select Committee that development planning should be focused on the improvements sought in children's learning. Within the guidance there is only one mention of checking the impact of planned developments on pupils' learning achievements.

Nevertheless, there began to be a perceived link between development planning, the expectation that schools were to be accountable institutions and the need to demonstrate effectiveness. The piecemeal introduction of the National Curriculum and arrangements for statutory assessment created pressure on schools to demonstrate how they intended to meet statutory requirements. Creating an order of priority in an SDP demonstrated that at least a school was taking account of its curriculum responsibilities, even if it was in no position to fulfil them.

The work of the School Management Task Force in 1990 also highlighted the importance of SDPs, but as a management tool rather than as a vehicle for improving learning. A development plan which included a management and staff development policy was perceived as characteristic of a successful school. This was shortly followed by the introduction of national arrangements for school inspection and a requirement that inspectors should judge the quality of the school development plan, but not its impact, and so the importance of the plan as a document in its own right was again underlined. 'The focus on school development planning as a vehicle for meeting a school's own self-review, evaluation and development purposes was realigned as it became perceived as an external measure of a school's effectiveness' (MacGilchrist *et al.* 1995).

The difficulty of a plan being translated into reality was, however, being recognized by the authors of the original DES school development planning guidance. In a follow-up booklet, Hargreaves and Hopkins recognized the difficulties created by spending too much time on the early stages of development planning. They suggested that a full-scale audit might be too time consuming – 'it might take 2–3 terms and only when it was completed would the development work for future years be planned' (DES 1991) – and they acknowledged that a small-scale audit might be more appropriate.

There was also a recognition that the implementation of plans was often the most difficult element in development planning. Having acknowledged this, the example of an action plan included in the guide is somewhat daunting, as it includes twenty-one tasks. There is, however, much more of a focus on school development planning being used as a vehicle to improve the quality of provision for pupils' learning.

The assumption of a link between the quality of a plan and school improvement was challenged by Ofsted in its report to the School Teachers' Review Body in 1993. Ofsted reported that the quality of SDPs had improved, but that there were still weaknesses in evaluating work in classrooms and in monitoring and evaluating standards achieved.

The changes in the use of school development planning as it attempted to meet the needs of a variety of groups and serve a range of purposes are highlighted in the three-year research study undertaken by the London University Institute of Education. The first chapter of *Planning Matters* (MacGilchrist *et al.* 1995) provides a useful overview of the growth of the SDP as a tool to enable schools to plan for curriculum and professional development, to be accountable for curriculum and budget management and to demonstrate an effective management structure. As the authors comment, these multiple and shifting purposes appear to be largely unquestioned, 'as does the perceived cause and effect relationship between planning for realistic development and demonstrating accountability.' Citing some of the issues which research in this area needs to take into account, the authors comment that

> the balance between the use of development planning to control the work of schools and the extent to which it can empower a school's own development will be a consideration not least because, increasingly, SDPs have become an innovation imported from outside. The relationship between a process – used as a management strategy to cope with multiple change – and the notion of development planning as a school improvement strategy will also need to be examined. So, too, will be the question of whether or not schools have been diverted too far from the original purpose of development planning, namely to improve the quality of pupil learning.
>
> (MacGilchrist *et al.* 1995)

Perhaps one of the most telling findings is that 'it is the head who has the most important part to play in getting the management arrangements right.'

The ways in which you might begin to get arrangements right are diverse and complex and, as we have tried to highlight, will depend to a large extent on the context within which you are working.

What is very clear is that the production of a plan which is perceived as a key task of the management of the school does not, of itself, lead to development.

There is a range of evidence which suggests that, despite a good deal of rhetoric, there is a very tenuous link between development planning and school improvement. The difficulty of implementing plans has already been cited and the potential for planning to make little or no impact within and throughout a school is highlighted in research. MacGilchrist *et al.* (1995) identified four main types of plan with distinct characteristics. The types range from the so-called rhetorical to a corporate plan. The rhetorical plan epitomizes the production of a plan in response to the perceived need to have one. There is no sense of ownership by either head or staff, the plan lacks clarity and purpose, the process of planning is not managed and, not surprisingly, the plan has a negative impact. The rhetorical plan is the type of plan written by an over-worked, over-tired head-teacher who feels the pressure to 'have a school development plan'. Producing the plan is seen as the end in itself, and the production is a task for the management. Teachers have very limited involvement and are largely ignorant of what the plan contains. The rhetorical plan bears very little relationship to what actually happens in the school. The corporate plan, by contrast, has as its key characteristic a shared sense of ownership, purpose and involvement. Teaching staff have a stake in the leadership and management of the process, and the plan, it is claimed, has a significant impact on school develop-ment, teacher development and pupils' learning. What this research confirms is that many schools are understandably confused about what precisely is expected of them in terms of development plan-ning. On the one hand they are being subjected to requests from LEAs and Ofsted to provide copies of the plan, by implication there-fore emphasizing the product. On the other hand researchers – in particular the school improvement lobby – are telling them that teacher participation and involvement are the most important aspects of planning, thereby emphasizing the process.

In relation to the planning process five key issues emerged from *Planning Matters*. What seemed to be important was that the planning process emanated from transformative leadership, that it was well managed, that the purpose was improvement in children's learning, that teachers felt a degree of involvement and ownership, and finally, and perhaps most importantly, that all these elements were shared by all staff. That research highlights these aspects of development goes some way to confirming our earlier assertions about the nature of educational leadership and how it is exercised. Our earlier ideas about leadership which is inclusive, embraces a range of opinions and actively seeks participation are all echoed in the research findings.

A new dimension, however, is the prominence given to the purpose of planning and the importance of maintaining a clear focus upon improving children's learning through teachers' development, and thereby improving teaching. MacGilchrist and her colleagues see a direct relationship between the focus on improvement and the process itself.

> However there was an added dimension to the focus. This was a distinct emphasis on bringing about improvements in pupils' learning. This focus, along with the quality of leadership and management of the plan and the process could well have accounted for the high level of teacher ownership and shared responsibility for the plan.
>
> (MacGilchrist *et al.* 1995)

The recent work on the impact of development planning and establishing a climate for school improvement (Ainscow and Hopkins 1994; MacGilchrist *et al.* 1995) contains some interesting messages for headteachers who wish to create a structure for genuine development which is clearly focused on enhancing pupils' opportunities for learning. Your role is pivotal in three key aspects of school management: managing the culture, developing strategic planning which is appropriate to your school and empowering staff. Clearly, all three are interlinked and to some extent interdependent.

What is very clear is that it is not the nature of a plan which brings about change but the nature of the process and the climate within which it is developed. Development planning will not of itself bring about change without other factors. If the development is going to be genuine then the nature of the process is far more critical than the nature of the plan. It is worth remembering that some of the most effective changes in schools may be unplanned and the result of force of circumstance or an unexpected opportunity. Development in these situations can only take place if schools, as we have said earlier, are fundamentally concerned with values and beliefs rather than structure and systems.

Perhaps the most interesting work in recent years on developing schools and individual teachers, which has very little to do with or say about school development planning, has been undertaken by Jennifer Nias and various colleagues in the course of several research projects.

For example, *Whole School Curriculum Development in the Primary School* (Nias *et al.* 1992), while concerned specifically with curriculum issues, clearly illustrates a range of circumstances in which develop-ment can occur at various levels. At one school spontaneous change took place following the provision of new resources and the initiative of one teacher which involved some colleagues in developing work in technology. At another, some teachers who sought to broaden the curriculum, and, for example, introduced open-ended enquiry into science lessons or made more use of the local environment to encourage creativity, had a particular impact on the curriculum in extending teachers' skills and thinking.

The key feature in all these types of development was the atti-tude of headteachers who created a climate in their schools which fostered questioning and a search for improvement within a climate of shared beliefs and sense of the school as a 'whole':

> the heads sought to foster a climate in which every aspect of the school, except its fundamental beliefs, was perceived as open to question and as capable of improvement . . . all heads encouraged their teachers to treat their choice of curriculum content and their pedagogy as open to question. In this sense curriculum development was a form of critical enquiry into current practice and future goals.
>
> (Nias *et al.* 1992)

Headteachers in Nias *et al.*'s study had a particular view of curricu-lum development, in that they felt a responsibility for the learning of each individual child and also had a set of educative beliefs on which practice could be built. The research provides illustrative examples of three aspects of curriculum development: creating a culture for change; establishing structures for development; and empowering staff. Establishing a sense of shared beliefs was in itself a devel-opmental activity and a key aspect of developing a whole-school identity. An added dimension to this was that the importance of creating a whole-school approach was balanced with a respect for the individuality of staff.

One of the important messages here is that there is no one form of development planning which is better than any other. The type of development can vary, and may result from a brief discussion at a staff meeting or may be represented in a detailed action plan. School development does not necessarily take place because it is endorsed in a written plan, and it may take place spontaneously. While the meaning of development may vary, the processes have some common characteristics.

The findings of Nias *et al.* (1992) preceded the study of school development planning led by MacGilchrist (1995) but share many of the elements of what is referred to as the corporate planning process. The whole-school approach, to which we shall return later, was underpinned by shared beliefs, attitudes and actions in relation to the aims and expectations of the school. Teachers had an awareness of their jobs which went beyond their own classrooms and a sense of having not only a contribution to make to the school as a whole but a responsibility to do so. A sense of shared purpose grew from a concern for the children and a view that what went on in school should be considered with their interests and needs in mind.

Teachers in the study (Nias *et al.* 1992) acknowledged their headteachers as effective leaders who held a clear set of beliefs but had the capacity to make allowances for individual differences. They also exercised leadership as part of a team. In considering this aspect of your leadership role, it is perhaps worth recalling that you, as a headteacher, are in a unique position. Only you can have an overview of all aspects of the school and take a 'whole-school' view. Teachers are inevitably concerned primarily with their activities in classrooms on a day-to-day basis and for some of them sharing responsibility for development, working together or opening up the practice for discussion or debate may be new or even threatening. As a headteacher you can be instrumental in creating a climate in which discussion, difference and even decisions are legitimized as part of an effective process of development.

The characteristics of successful development illustrate the point that development can be taking place in a variety of ways at different levels simultaneously and that it does not necessarily follow a linear pattern. In the schools studied by Nias *et al.* (1992) development was often gradual and the teachers involved needed to feel that change would benefit their pupils and not interfere with their freedom to select and teach in ways which they would find acceptable. The change had to become part of their thinking and an initiative only became part of their practice if they felt it would not impose unreasonable constraints on the ways in which they worked.

This notion of 'ownership' is one which occurs frequently in the literature on successful change. Ainscow and Hopkins (1994) cite the importance of establishing a climate which encourages genuine participation by staff in improvement, and the need to establish 'management arrangements that empower': 'A commitment to participate in the leadership process seems to grow from the headteacher's commitment to secure participation – once staff believe the intention is genuine then the quality of individual involvement increases' (Ainscow and Hopkins 1994). We referred in Chapter 3 to the importance of school culture in a climate for change. The leadership role of the head in creating a whole-school approach to development is a critical one. There is a fine balance to be struck between facilitating the participation and empowerment of staff, and at times using one's authority in an effort to establish or retain a common set of beliefs and continuing to provide an educational vision for the school (Nias *et al.* 1992).

The creation of conditions under which teachers can learn and work together is fundamental to bringing about a climate for change. Fullan (1992) cites the importance of a professional culture in schools which is based on a sense of collegiality. He uses the term 'interactive professionalism', which is described as simultaneously a strategy and an outcome of leadership. Again, creating a culture in which there is genuine collaboration, an openness to new ideas and a focus on instructional improvement echoes the themes of successful development cited elsewhere (see Nias *et al.* 1989; Reynolds and Cutlance 1992).

The views of teachers about whole-school cultures clearly demonstrate the inherent tension between establishing organizational strategies and systems and empowering staff. Nias (1989) identified some common beliefs about the nature of a 'whole school'. Teachers felt that

- each member of the staff group belonged to a community;
- they shared common educational beliefs and aims and interpreted these in similar ways;
- they worked together as a team;
- they exercised autonomy in their own classrooms;
- they related well to each other;
- their knowledge of and concern about the school went beyond their own classes to encompass the concerns and practices of colleagues;
- they valued the leadership of the head.

The ways in which you may need to function in order to bring about development and improvement will depend, as with so many other aspects of school leadership, on the context within which you are endeavouring to work. Undoubtedly there are certain organizational, professional and interpersonal conditions which seem to facilitate professional learning, and it is that learning and the opportunity for professional growth which underlie successful development.

The quality of professional relationships and opportunities for professional interaction are fundamental to development at an individual and whole-school level. The forms of professional interaction undertaken by teachers in Nias's study make interesting reading, in that they reveal that it is often the tangible, task-sharing activities which begin to build a collaborative culture. So planning a perform-ance, organizing a school journey and sorting out resources are as much a strategy for interaction as being a member of a policy working group or leading school-based INSET. Professional relationships, and these would go beyond teachers to include support staff, governors, parents and pupils, set the tone for openness, teamwork and pro-fessional support as well as illustrating a respect for the professional judgement and autonomy of individual teachers. Obviously the degree to which staff collaborate is indicative of their professional commitment to the whole school, but there is a tension between an approach which promotes a sense of whole-school responsibility and individual teachers' sense of commitment to their own classes.

The organizational arrangements and structures of a school are important elements in beginning to resolve some of these tensions. The definition of responsibilities, the processes for decision-making and a system for communication need to be explicit if teachers are to feel a commitment to any form of development. While establish-ing such structures, you will need to define the ways in which individual teachers can have a stake in decisions made and raise any issues concerned with both individual classroom practice and the school as a whole. If classroom practice is to improve and there is to be a genuine improvement in opportunities for pupils' learn-ing, then staff development needs to be located in classrooms. Oppor-tunities for learning need to embrace adults as well as children. The notion of a school as a learning community is an indicator of the prevailing culture.

The recent study by the National Commission on Education (1996) on effective schools in disadvantaged areas reinforces the messages about school culture, teamwork and commitment as the basis of successful development. Schools which were successful had clearly defined a context for their work based on the community they served, their history and existing strengths. There was a focus on the positive aspects of the school and schools defined their own priorities, regardless of national imperatives. These priorities were limited in number, with three or four areas being the focus for development at any one time. Three features emerged as common characteristics underpinning successful development:

- ◆ a collaborative culture was established for staff and pupils;
- ◆ the role of the learner was defined, which included establishing a shared view of good work and standards of behaviour;
- ◆ schools celebrated improvement and gave pupils a sense of self-worth.

Perhaps most telling were the characteristics of the headteachers who led the schools whom Margaret Maden, a member of the National Commission, described as 'aiming for the future perfect with relentless optimism' (ASPE Conference, 5 October 1996).

As we have already said, development is not necessarily planned, sequential or rational in a linear sense, but may be opportunistic and spontaneous. That is not to deny the importance of planned development and the validity of planning to prioritize initiatives and responses at a variety of levels. Indeed, Fullan (1991) illustrated that 'starting small and thinking big' can help with sequencing priorities and building on existing good practice wherever it might be found. In that way, successful leaders can shape conditions to influence the developing school culture, and this again is illustrated by the National Commission's study.

Any planning mechanism, however, needs to be sufficiently flexible to take account of changes, opportunities and distractions. The huge number of factors that may influence or distract from a planned development have already been discussed and are neatly summarized by Nias (1989).

> Primary schools are constantly changing, in unpredictable ways. Teachers' classroom lives were changing, almost by the minute, number of adults (teaching, ancillary and support, visiting, part-time volunteers, full-time) daily came and went from the head's office, the staffroom and the school, their mood and their numbers affected by predictable events (such as in-service courses) and unpredictable ones (such as illness or vandalism), the tempo, rhythm and content of school life altered with the seasons and in response to specific events (such as medical inspections and fire drills). The feelings and energy levels of headteachers and staff rose and fell, following the dictates of their personal lives as well as of events in school. More dramatically, staff left, requiring the attention of those who remained to be focused upon replacing them, upon the subsequent socialisation of newcomers and upon their own accommodation to new colleagues and fresh ideas. These constant modifications to the personnel, tasks, climate and feelings of the staff created an endemic potential for disequilibrium within each school.
>
> (Nias 1989)

Schools are dynamic, not static, institutions. Destabilization or internal turbulence can occur for a number of reasons; if schools are genuinely to develop, then as much energy and attention needs to be paid to creating a culture for change as to putting together a detailed and beautifully documented development plan. Development planning is no more than a framework within which to operate. As a headteacher you will need to decide whether the school development planning is to provide a management tool which provides a sense of direction for the school and acts as a safety net in identifying a list of areas for development over a period of time, or whether it is to be a process of which all sectors of the school community have knowledge and to which they have access. If the latter is the case, then the written manifestation of the plan is of secondary value to its formulation.

5

DEFINING THE

PURPOSE

This chapter will forge links between some of the different themes we have looked at so far and attempt to show how primary headteachers can begin to bring to life their ideas in conjunction with the ideas of others. We have looked at the concept of leadership (and indeed teaching) as a reflective practice on the part of the practitioner. Reflective practice can continue to occur – helpfully or otherwise – *ad nauseam*, but if it is going to contribute to the work of a school then it must be directed. In this sense, the reflection needs to be harnessed to an aim, or, in the current jargon, contribute to the vision that the community has for its school. To bring together the various aspects of reflection within the orbit of a shared vision is also to begin to create and work within the school's particular culture. This notion of simultaneously creating, developing and enhancing a school's culture and working within it is complex. It is important to understand that the processes which a school goes through in defining its purpose are an expression of its culture, while at the same time demonstrating a determination to recreate the culture. It is the nature of this process and how it might be undertaken which this chapter will address.

The vision that any community might have for its school will have several characteristics. Simply to define a vision, for example, in terms of improving National Curriculum assessment results reduces the vision to a set of statistics, but it also grounds it in reasonably concrete terms. At the other end of the spectrum, to define vision in terms of all individual children reaching their full potential is to render it almost meaningless and thereby uncontentious. Defining a vision which is meaningful will inevitably mean including areas which are contentious.

While a vision may express an idealized version, or a dream to which the school aspires, it must also express some commitments.

No one would disagree that each child should reach his or her full potential, because the statement has very limited meaning in a practical sense. It begs the question of what exactly potential is and how we define it, and makes absolutely no reference to what the implications of such a statement might be. To carry the hopes and aspirations of a community, to provide that community with the purpose and the context for its activity, a vision must touch the community and inspire it through an appeal to those elements of life which on the one hand go far beyond academic success, but on the other articulate values and beliefs which are demonstrable and provide a framework for the school's activities. As Starratt (1990) eloquently writes,

> the vision has its roots in those deep, core meanings about human life, its dignity, grandeur, beauty, value etc. . . . It is concerned with values such as freedom, honour, selflessness, loyalty, devotion to community, integrity and dignity of the person, equality, peace and harmony among peoples, the rule of law, the elevation of reason and civility, wisdom, self-governance, courage, character, a perfect performance, creative expression, harmony with nature etc.

These ideas are not unfamiliar, but do not conform to the lexicon of the management consultant. Such a vision would touch the heart of schooling, but would also require skill, knowledge and understanding to achieve. As Starratt goes on to say,

> A vision of education, if it is to be anything more than a collection of prescribed platitudes about schools must be grounded in those meanings basic to human life . . . It does require . . . that educators reflect on what they believe to be the values and meanings basic to human life, and that they reflect on whether they practise those beliefs in their work in the school.

To think of a vision in this way has some significant implications in terms of both the nature and characteristics of leaders and the preparedness of the community to accept an element of conflict. If you are to regard a vision for the school as something as fundamental as Starratt clearly does, then you must have the determination and courage to try to influence the nature and content of the vision, while at the same time understanding that conflict may be a semi-permanent condition. To try to get an entire community to agree upon such a vision is difficult and time consuming, and is a process which needs careful thought. It also needs leaders to act with what Fullan (1992) refers to as 'fearlessness'. He makes very clear that this notion is not akin to foolishess, but nevertheless requires courage, determination and an element of risk taking. Headteachers operate in an increasingly prescribed world and it is important that risk taking retains a degree of legitimacy. The very act of striving to achieve a vision should go some way to encouraging heads to be 'fearless'. Once in place, the vision encourages fearlessness by enabling schools to function with reference to the vision and to have the courage to say no occasionally to developments and initiatives which do not go towards reaching that vision.

Conflict is an almost inevitable consequence of a vision which is concerned with values. If such a vision involves no conflict then we may be agreeing about motherhood and apple pie or we may be sleepwalking. Remember, leadership needs to be reflective and critical in the sense that educators sometimes need to search out areas of disagreement, encourage a degree of scepticism and face difficult questions – particularly from those new to the school. That is not to say that the vision is not unifying, it is to say that it is fluid and complex, it accepts the idea that different factors can and do emerge. The vision will always be subject to a range of perspectives and not every element of the vision will have universal approval. Teachers, governors, children and parents should all understand the vision, but each will have his or her particular and specific element to which he or she is especially allied. What we need to explore is what the vision might include, and how it might be generated and articulated.

If the vision is to make the kind of impact it should, if it is to command support and ensure commitment, then it has to inspire and motivate. It must express the ideal together with the possibility of attainment. It must provide the guiding framework for school activity, but must also put the activity within a context. There are two ways of approaching the building of a vision. For some schools there is a desire to try to encapsulate their own particular vision in a short sentence or paragraph which can be used almost as a motto. There is nothing wrong with this approach, but if a 'catchy phrase' or the 'mission statement' is the starting point it can lead to an initial overemphasis upon the wording and phrasing of the statement without the benefit of wider discussions. If, at the end of the process, the school feels it appropriate to produce a mission statement for use in the prospectus or other documents, then fine – but we would urge that the vision should emerge from considerable discussion and argument. The agenda for the discussion has to be concerned with those aspects of schooling which we have already explored. It must include some broad agreement about the nature and purpose of education and the specific part that this school will play in that purpose. In a sense this is about the intentions, but it must also engage in the processes and begin to describe a view of how those intentions are to be realized. As this is concerned with major issues, it needs to be practicable and it needs some organization. It may, however, be helpful in the first instance to think carefully about the particular components of the vision. We suggest that a vision for a school should encompass broad agreements about the following:

- the nature and purpose of education;
- the nature of the school's curriculum;
- the working relationships within school;
- the way the school relates to its community.

A word of caution at this stage may be helpful. It is important to bear in mind the purpose of this exercise, and perhaps that can be most effectively stated by saying what it is not. The purpose is not to produce two or three sides of A4 paper to satisfy Ofsted or anyone else. The purpose is to inspire and enthuse a group of people through generating a picture of what they might achieve together. It is about providing a meaning to working lives, and giving a sense of purpose and coherence to a range of varied activities. As we have said, if at some point a school wishes to record its vision, then fine, but this is not the main purpose. Bearing this in mind, we can now move on to looking in a little more detail at each of the components and what they might include.

THE NATURE AND PURPOSE OF EDUCATION

If a school is to have a coherent purpose, if its activities are to be seen as a whole and if it is to achieve a degree of consistency, then it must be underpinned by a shared educational philosophy. This is not a fashionable view, since teachers are now being repeatedly urged to abandon the philosophical rhetoric of progressive education and return to basic skills taught in a common-sense sort of way. Simply because the currently favoured alternative to progressive education is referred to as 'common sense' or 'basic skills' in no way diminishes it from being an expression of a philosophy of education, since the advocates of these approaches are as much ideologists as the de-schoolers.

To say that a practice emanates from something called common sense rather than a philosophy is merely to change the name. As Carr (1995) points out, 'Questions arise about how the choice of teaching methods is justified, about the purposes that the selected curriculum content serves and – if this line of questioning is pushed far enough – about what precisely education is being taken to mean.' It is therefore important that those involved in a school have a shared view of what we mean by education. We must be clear, however, about the contested nature of the meaning of this term. In one sense we all know what we mean by the concept of education, but we may disagree about the conception of education. The 1988 Education Act, and the changes it brought about, result from a particular conception of education. Similarly, the current assessment arrangements reflect a conception of education in the same way that those who advocate child-centredness and children learning through discovery are declaring a conception of education. If we persist in asking enough questions about why schools and teachers do as they do, then we end with being offered a particular view of what a good society or a good life might mean. In other words, conceptions of education are often rooted in a politics and the political traditions of Britain all have their particular conceptions of education.

If any educational practice is to be meaningful, rather than a series of unconnected meaningless events, then it must be grounded in some view of education. It may not be referred to grandly as philosophy, but nevertheless a school's practice is manifesting a specific conception of education. So the choice for a school engaged in the business of creating a vision is not to decide whether or not to have a philosophy of education, but to decide what that philosophy is to be. In making these kinds of decisions schools are laying the foundation stones of the vision they want to establish, they are providing the context and parameters of the vision. It is important at this stage not to get too bogged down with practice, but to maintain and develop a picture of what ultimately the school is striving to achieve. Developing practice will be dictated by the chosen philosophy and ultimately be matched against the rhetoric of the vision.

Deciding on what philosophy will underpin the vision is not easy. It touches very fundamental issues and can therefore be threatening and unsettling. However, and this is an important point to bear in mind, there are countless examples of schools in which the participants share a largely similar outlook about what they are doing. This is not the result of a purposeful series of meetings in which the staff debate and decide on their particular philosophy. It is often due to the development of aspects of teaching which implicitly make similar assumptions about the way things are done. In other words, teachers will often develop a shared philosophy by doing things together and in this sense the philosophy will be implicit. In our view, it would seem to be beneficial for the implicit to be made explicit, as that would enable everyone to make assumptions with confidence. It would ensure that discussions about practice could be referred to the school's philosophy and allow schools to develop and grow according to their own values and beliefs. It would also give a better opportunity for a school to achieve a greater degree of compatibility between its philosophy and practice.

To point out that everything a school does is underpinned by its philosophy may be true, but it is not particularly helpful in identifying a strategy which a school might use to articulate its own particular philosophy. It is more helpful to try to answer a question about the basic elements in an educational philosophy. What are the aspects of schooling on which it is fundamental for a school to state its position? To answer this may be to provide some framework by which schools can identify, develop and articulate their unique philosophy. To attempt to answer the question 'What is the purpose of education?' will necessitate an engagement with those ideas which form the two major traditions of British schooling. On the one hand there is the traditional conservative perspective, which highlights academic excellence and the education of an elite group, with the determined segregation of children by ability. At the other end of the spectrum, the liberal tradition would highlight the needs of individual children, the education of the whole child and children being grouped together in flexible ways. These traditions implicitly express markedly different educational purposes. The traditional perspective would point to the need to educate an elite to a high standard and the importance of equipping everyone with the skills with which to make a living. This utilitarian view of education contrasts sharply with the progressive ideas about equality of opportunity and the belief that education should be life enhancing and go beyond the acquisition of necessary skills. The above represents two extremes, and the reality is that both traditions share some key ideas, and that, in Carr's (1995) phrase, they 'often merge and overlap'. Despite this frequent convergence, the traditions do represent a range of practice and structure about which any school must make decisions. Once a school has a clear and shared view on what the main purposes of education are, it can begin to see in a clearer way other elements of the vision. So the question for all schools is: what is the school trying to teach? Any response to this must articulate a balance between the academic and the social and must explore the relationship between individual fulfilment and collective responsibility. The school must define its purpose in terms of the knowledge, skills and understanding that children will acquire, while at the same time teaching them to relate to others, become responsible and develop the ability to contribute to the life of the community.

One possible way of opening up this kind of discussion is to focus upon children. It is a useful exercise to try to describe the qualities, attributes and characteristics which you would wish for the children when they reach the end of their school life. If the school is successful, what will the children be like when they leave? This exercise can be facilitated by producing life-size outlines of children and asking teachers (and others) to describe their aspirations for children in terms of personal qualities, social qualities and academic achievement. As groups complete their 'pictures', a process of negotiation and editing will provide some ideas about what the school is trying to teach. Whatever the decision about purposes, they will have a direct impact upon the nature of provision and it is this aspect of the vision that we will move on to.

THE NATURE OF THE CURRICULUM

To a large extent the nature of a school's curriculum will flow naturally from its educational philosophy, since in some respects the curriculum is the outward manifestation of a school's philosophy. This is not to imply, however, that decisions do not have to be taken. It would be useful at this point to clarify what we mean by curriculum. Quite simply, a school's curriculum is taken to encompass all the planned activities and arrangements with which the school is engaged. This wider definition would therefore include not just the academic taught curriculum, but also embrace the pastoral arrangements and the various policies concerning behaviour and the school's approach to personal and social development. It would involve decisions about approaches to special educational needs and the nature of assessment arrangements. It would also be concerned with educational process as much as content and therefore have some bearing upon the arrangements for grouping children. As can be seen, this is a sizable agenda which gets to the heart of what schools are about. This element of the vision is probably that which gets closest to the everyday experiences of teachers and children, but at this stage it is crucial to bear in mind that we are not planning a school's curriculum. What we are doing is creating a picture of a curriculum which would emanate from a given set of curriculum principles. It is the principles which must be established, and this can be accomplished through addressing a series of questions, the answers to which would begin to build up a framework on which to base the curriculum. Such a series of questions could include the following.

♦ Does the curriculum represent a common entitlement?
♦ What is the content of the curriculum?
♦ What is the nature of children's learning?

To put these questions into some kind of context, we can return to the conservative and liberal traditions mentioned above to map out the territory.

If we consider how the conservative tradition responds to the first question we are able to identify one end of the spectrum. The curriculum as a common entitlement is not within this particular tradition, since it is more concerned to identify a range of curricula which may be suitable or appropriate for a range of children. Hence the distinction between the academic, vocational and technical curriculum. It is ironic that a Conservative government has introduced a curriculum – the National Curriculum – which does represent a common entitlement and which is not within the conservative tradition. At the present time, however, the moves to increase a school's facility to select a proportion of its intake and the creation of city technology colleges indicate that the tradition is alive and kicking and is represented in the themes of 'choice and diversity' at the heart of current policy. In terms of curriculum content, the conservative tradition would emphasize knowledge rather than process and see the curriculum as a body of knowledge to be transmitted. Education would be a process which passed down knowledge with the purpose of educating children into a tradition to enable them to uphold it. Within this conservative tradition, knowledge is less contestable and is characterized by claims to objective fact. This view of the curriculum reflects ideas about the ways in which children learn. The curriculum is seen as a body of knowledge to be transmitted, and children are vessels into which the knowledge is poured. Learning is, from this perspective, a passive activity in which children are given information which is assimilated through practice and consolidation.

In contrast, the liberal tradition offers a view of the curriculum which is broad and represents a common entitlement. Children would have an equal opportunity to partake in a liberal curriculum, which would include an engagement with all aspects of knowledge. Knowledge itself would encompass attitudes and feelings and an appeal to human sensibilities, and, put crudely, the liberal tradition would claim that to engage with this book, that play, these ideas will improve and develop the human condition. While being concerned to transmit a cultural tradition, it would also maintain that knowledge is much more contestable, and would embrace subjectivity and indeed, in more recent times, relativism. In the liberal tradition, learning is an active process in which children participate in a deliberate and purposeful way. Carr (1995) has characterized both these traditions by their derivation from the texts of Plato's *Republic* and Rousseau's *Emile*.

Neither of these extreme ends of the educational spectrum would accurately represent a school's curriculum. Most schools would in the current jargon 'cherry pick' ideas from each of the traditions. In other words, most schools would have a regard to the personal and social discussions of the liberal tradition as well as some sympathy with the implicit understanding of the nature of children's learning which encourages activity and exploration. At the same time, however, no school will ignore the importance of knowledge and the critical need for all children to acquire 'the basic skills'.

Implicit, however, within these two extreme views of the curriculum are the regimes under which the curriculum should be taught, which in turn will impact upon pastoral systems and the involvement, or not, of children in the setting of rules and the nature of punishments. Essentially, decisions will have to be made about the balance between rights and responsibilities, both for children and for staff. These decisions would be concerned with justice and equal opportunities and how these affect the way children are taught. To begin to consider these issues leads naturally into the next area which informs the school's vision.

THE WORKING RELATIONSHIPS WITHIN SCHOOL

We can begin to explore the possibilities of what the nature of relationships may be within a school from various perspectives. One starting point is to remind ourselves of some of the features of leadership which we discussed above. The particular features of leadership which would have a direct bearing upon the school's relationships are those which regard leadership as both ethical and educative. These features should underpin the nature of the relationships, and imply a second starting point, which picks up the notion from above, of rights and responsibilities. If leadership is to be ethical and educative then there must be a vision of the rights and responsibilities of all those engaged in the work of the school. Further chapters will explore some of the practical implications of these ideas, but it is important that the vision includes an inspiring and motivating picture of how people can expect to be treated. In this context, therefore, what might be the ethical considerations which should underpin relationships? We could begin by reiterating the view that, first and foremost, people will not be seen as a means to someone else's ends. This implies leadership which is embracing in character rather than isolated, and is genuine in the desire to negotiate ends and means. Such a leadership places significant rights and responsibilities upon the leader and the led. Those who are led have rights such as those to be heard, to be consulted and to be informed. Reciprocal responsibilities on the part of the leader would be to listen, consult and inform. Those who are leaders would also have rights in terms of what they can expect of those who are led. Leaders could expect others to assist their own learning and maintain an informed view of aspects of school life, they could expect a degree of commitment and responsibility to the school. Such leadership does not simply bestow rights upon the led. If the led are to engage with leadership, then they must accept a significant degree of responsibility. Those responsibilities should be taken seriously, as a denial of them could put the enterprise at risk. Consider the analogy quoted by Inglis (1989) of the democratic right to vote. If people do not accept the responsibility of exercising their right then democracy is put at risk. As he succinctly puts it, people may have to be forced to be free; hence in Australia it is a legal requirement to vote in general elections.

To create a vision of working relationships means addressing rights and responsibilities, but it also means thinking carefully about where power may be located and the nature of decision-making. These are difficult but important areas, since they anticipate and assume conflict, unless the only decisions made are those which enjoy a consensus. Always to seek consensus can lead to a lack of progress and a cycle of unproductive meetings which schools find it difficult to break, although on the surface they appear to be schools which are content. Any vision must therefore anticipate conflict, together with some notion of how conflict may be resolved. There is a view, prevalent within primary schools, that conflict is something to be avoided at all costs, that it signifies a breakdown in relationships and is always unproductive. This view actually flies in the face of most people's realities and it is important that conflict be recognized as an important element within schools which are concerned with improvement and, as is pointed out in Chapter 3, it is almost an inevitable consequence of change.

If a key element in leadership is that it is educative, what does that mean in terms of working relationships? Again this involves being reasonably specific about the rights and responsibilities which fall upon leaders and the led. Leadership which purports to be educative must exhibit a determination to offer all staff opportunities to learn. It must have learning as a central concern which embraces teachers as well as children. Educative leadership has a responsibility to widen horizons, encourage critical awareness and support the reflective dimension of the educational process. It must also accept the responsibility of being prepared to enter the debate and engage with a variety of views and opinions. As a backdrop to these responsibilities, educative leadership must exhibit wisdom and patience and accept the responsibilities for other people's failures. Once again though, this is not one-way traffic. Educative leadership has the right to expect an active response from all staff. That response could include a willingness on the part of staff to engage in debate, a preparedness to explore and reflect upon the complexities of the job and a commitment to improvement.

What is being proposed here is a framework of rights and responsibilities which embraces everyone in the purpose and vision of the school. This is in contrast to the currently perceived necessity to write job descriptions which articulate the current list of functions, responsibilities and tasks, but are ultimately designed to be just another aspect of managerial surveillance. (Job descriptions are seen as the key document of any appraisal system – if we don't know what you're supposed to do, how can we decide if you're doing it?) A framework of relationships, as we propose it, has the school's endeavours at its heart. Those who work in the school share a set of aspirations and it is to the aspirations – or the vision – that they commit themselves. It is through the commitment to the school that they take responsibility and accept particular rights. It is responsibility that is both personal and public which is at the heart of this particular community of teachers. This expansive and inclusive notion leads us into the final element which will assist us in defining our school vision.

HOW THE SCHOOL RELATES TO THE COMMUNITY

This is a further aspect of schooling on which there are a range of conflicting ideas, but any vision of schooling must encompass some perspective of how the school interacts with its local community. For the purposes of this, local community refers particularly to parents, although this is not to ignore other identifiable groups of people, such as senior citizens, local businesses and other community-based organizations, which are often legitimately regarded as part of the local community by schools. The definition of local community is not a contentious issue here; rather the community will define itself as a consequence of the vision of the relationships which a school adopts.

The marketization and commodification of education has encouraged the view that a school relates to its community in the same way as a business relates to its customers. It is essentially the view that parents are consumers of a product and as consumers have a right to certain information about the various products on offer – hence the parents' charter. Subsequent to having this information, they are free to choose where to cash in their right to education. What this leads to is schools becoming increasingly concerned with public relations and all that that manifests in terms of school brochures, marketing and of course league tables of test results. This narrow commercial view of schools and their communities is putting a considerable strain upon many schools, since it is not an accurate reflection of the value system many understand to be at the heart of education. This market relationship between home and school, while often referred to as a partnership, is not a partnership of equals. It is a partnership in which the customer is increasingly seen as right and it is a partnership which at its heart divides home and school into separate camps. It is another example of the non-sequitor at the core of the thinking of the New Right, that partnerships can be built between groups which at the same time are being pushed apart in the name of market forces. This is a barren and brutal vision of educational partnerships which has no feeling for a school as part of a community, a school which accepts and responds to its responsibilities to serve, not as a provider, but as an institution deeply embedded within the life of its community.

To paint a picture of what this might look like is to delve more into the palette of family life and to begin to see what part a school might play in the life of its families. If education is both a lifelong and a family concern, then a school can begin to respond to the needs of families through supporting and enhancing family opportunities. This inevitably will mean forging networks and building new partnerships with other agencies and establishments. Community education is a seamless web which responds to the particular needs of a community by becoming part of the community. In many areas of the country, schools have transformed people's lives through providing experiences and opportunities which have made an impact upon adults and children. We will return to aspects of this part of the vision, particularly the relationship with parents, in a later chapter, but suffice it to say at the moment that what is offered here is in marked contrast to the vision implicit within the notion of education as a commodity.

To summarize briefly at this point, we have looked closely at the importance to the school of having a vision and explored what the components of such a vision might include. As the headteacher you will find yourself with a paradox. On the one hand you will feel (rightly) the responsibility of articulating the vision, since that is why you were appointed, but you also know that on the other hand you must offer a vision which is to be shared. In this sense the head-teacher's job is to orchestrate the vision, to provide opportunities for the vision to develop, to coordinate and balance the inevitably varying points of view. As Starratt (1990) puts it,

> When a staff works together under the inspiration and motiva-
> tion of a shared vision, leadership is a quality that all on the
> staff begin to exercise ... Leaders try to keep the community
> focused on the vision because the power for greatness comes
> not from the leader but from the communal vision of greatness.

All headteachers must come to terms with the above paradox. While any vision, if it is to have meaning, must be shared, the task of creating the vision cannot realistically involve everyone all the time. In other words, the process of visioning needs to be thought about and organized in such a way that everyone feels involved and all have opportunities to contribute without it becoming an endless series of discussions. There is a second dilemma which is worth mentioning. To begin to discuss, think and perhaps argue about a vision may put some possible strain on people's relationships. This would suggest that appropriate relationships are established prior to the visioning. However, it would be our view that 'the medium is the message', in the sense that the process itself should make a positive contribution to developing the relationships. To some extent it depends upon the context. If as a new headteacher you begin this process, then it is a good way of exploring the web of relationships while at the same time giving a clear indication of your own position *vis-à-vis* the nature of the way the school is run. If you are a more experienced headteacher embarking on such a process, then you will inevitably have a history with which to contend and will have to organize the process accordingly in such a way that it may change the nature of the relationships which currently exist.

Another aspect of visioning which it is important to remember is that it is not some kind of daydream created by a headteacher, or anyone else, sitting comfortably in an armchair. It has to be grounded in some kind of reality and must confront many everyday issues of life in schools. It is through the 'picture' of the ideal that a school will be enabled to set its own goals, to which it can aspire over a period of time.

The process can be organized in various ways, but the following suggested strategies have been used successfully by several schools. The intention is to offer everyone an opportunity to think about those aspects of schooling highlighted above. To do this a school needs to provide time. Staff development days provide an excellent opportunity, especially if two can be put together to create a two-day residential conference so that staff have an opportunity to relax, yet maintain informal discussions. As opinions are sought, and offered, there needs to be sensitivity to the fact that not everyone will be comfortable about volunteering opinions in large groups, so again this needs careful organization. What follows is a possible structure to assist a school in developing its own vision over a period of time. As we go through the process the 'commentary' will highlight key aspects which need to be considered. As an example we will focus upon that aspect of the vision which is concerned with the nature of the relationships within school.

Initially the headteacher needs to give a clear indication of what is going to happen. Some background information about the process will contextualize the activity, but most importantly it must create the atmosphere in which people feel sufficiently secure and motivated to contribute to the vision. This introductory session must ensure that there is an emphasis upon the practical nature of the task and how much it is rooted in reality. There is a danger that otherwise the process will be seen as being unconnected with what actually happens and will perhaps be perceived as rather impractical. The next step is to gather opinions and ensure that everyone can make a contribution. A useful way of doing this is to provide a series of statements for people to complete. These statements are an important element, as they are the beginning of the creation of the picture. In our example, statements which relate to the nature of the relationships could be the following:

I want to work with a headteacher who . . .

I want to work with teachers who . . .

As a teacher I want to have opportunities for . . .

I want a staffroom where . . .

As a teacher I want to work with support staff . . .

I want to support teachers who . . .

In the first instance these statements should be printed individually on pieces of paper and freely available so that people can complete the same statements in different ways without having to discuss the issues with anyone else. After a period of time, staff should be encouraged to discuss their responses in pairs and, depending on the size of the group, pairs could eventually join together in fours. As they discuss their own responses the process should lead to editing or summarizing of the responses, so that duplication is avoided and perhaps new responses are generated which encapsulate the ideas of several individuals. As this proceeds and statements are completed, they should be publicly displayed so that at the end of this session or sessions what has been created is a large display of many completed statements which begin to describe the nature of the working relationships people desire. Everyone should be encouraged to read all the statements and collectively begin to sort and classify them into groups, which may say similar things or be different responses to the same statement. As the statements and responses are sorted, further editing can take place until finally each section can be reduced to a manageable number of statements which fairly represent the range of responses offered. Clearly this is a lengthy process involving several meetings or a significant part of a development day. It is, however, an effective way of ensuring that everyone has the opportunity to contribute and that discussions are very much focused upon key aspects of school life. It also begins to open up and confront values and attitudes, as these are inevitably implicit within the statements. In a sense these statements at this stage will represent a vision, but it is necessary to go further. As each section of the display is edited and distilled more needs to be done to create the picture of what in practice such a vision would look like. This involves more discussion, but by this stage small groups could work upon particular statements and present their ideas to the larger group; in other words, not everyone needs to be involved in everything at this stage, but everyone must be involved in something. Once again, printed sheets are a useful way of guiding people's thoughts. Following our examples, it is quite conceivable that something close to the following statements may emerge:

I want to work with teachers who collaborate and support each other.

I want to work with a headteacher who consults people and
listens to different opinions.

What needs to be done at this point is begin to create the reality
of what such a vision would actually mean. In other words, what
would the first statement mean in practice? Using this as a starting
point groups or pairs could put 'flesh on to the bones'.

I want to work with teachers who collaborate and support each
other.

In practice this means . . .

In some ways, it is at this point that the real visioning occurs. It is
very much akin to painting a picture, an opportunity to describe the
really possible rather than just articulating some grand sounding
statements which cannot be grounded or fixed in everyday practice.
By describing how an aspiration might be translated into reality, the
school is setting its goals and providing a clearly articulated sense of
direction. It is also ensuring a real chance that the vision is a shared
one, that people have a stake in working towards achieving their
aspirations.

To begin to define what something means in practice not only
puts 'flesh on the bones' but also begins to define the nature of relationships, and will indicate the range of rights and responsibilities
which various members of the school community carry. This close
scrutiny of shared aspirations delves into people's values and attitudes
and, if done sensitively, should create a vision which is not shared
rhetoric but has the credibility of being practical and achievable.

This process can be applied to each of those elements which go
to make up the school's vision. At different points, different people
will become involved, including children, governors and groups
of parents. While this process is to some extent an intimate one,
larger scale activities such as questionnaires can also be used to seek
the range of opinions from different groups. As the vision is created,
so it can be shared.

As headteacher, in creating such a vision you will open up valuable lines of communication and will have ample opportunity to
express your own ideas about the future. You will have articulated
your own values and attitudes while at the same time learning a
great deal about everyone else's. This process may not make the
job of being a headteacher any easier, but it does make it more
coherent and meaningful. It will give everyone not only direction
and purpose but, through the wisdom of the headteacher, a degree
of confidence. During this chapter we have used as an example of

visioning the nature of the relationships within the school. To some extent, this was a deliberate decision to highlight this aspect as central to how a school operates. While the vision will provide the broad overview of these relationships, what we will begin to do at this stage is to explore in more detail those components which go to make up successful working relationships.

6

WORKING WITH

STAFF

This chapter will explore some of the key relationships within school. It will focus particularly upon the nature of the relationships between the headteacher and teaching and non-teaching staff. We will pick up many of the earlier themes, particularly those in Chapter 3, and attempt to define what relationships may look like in the light of the democratic values and attitudes outlined in that chapter. The chapter will also try to set working relationships within the context of the school culture which such relationships would produce.

What will emerge in this chapter is a complex picture which contrasts sharply with the sometimes simple and naive ideas of managerialism. A major weakness inherent within managerialism is its claims to be able to predict events, the idea that if one thing happens – a decision is made, for instance – then the rest will follow. What this chapter will try to reflect is the subjective, less predictable way in which primary schools work, while showing how a shared vision can guide a more realistic and honest approach to the realities of working in a school. The starting point for the chapter is the vision of relationships touched upon in the previous chapters, which in turn reflects the values inherent within some of the more radical and democratic views of leadership.

It would be helpful to start to make more explicit some of the connections between earlier ideas, particularly those which focused upon the nature of leadership and the vision of leadership, and the vision of relationships based upon rights and responsibilities. What is being proposed here is that we can begin to think about what responsibilities you as headteacher, and indeed other leaders in the school, may have towards staff given the particular nature of educational leadership. If we accept that educational leadership should be educative, transformative, critical and ethical, then what are the responsibilities of headship? In a sense a headteacher, to use McLuhan's famous phrase, has to be the medium and the message. Not only must you embody these attributes of leadership, you must also encourage, develop and initiate those attributes among the staff to the extent that ultimately they become characteristic of the school. After all, it should be appropriate to describe a school as critical, transforming, educative and ethical. Such a view carries with it a pattern of relationships and specific responsibilities on the part of the headteacher. To attempt to describe those responsibilities is difficult, however, because they are also deeply embedded within, and help to create, the school atmosphere or culture. We need to identify both the modes of behaviour which will stem from your responsibilities, and the climate in which the behaviour might take place, although we know that each contributes to the other.

To be critical as a headteacher, you must have an acute awareness and understanding both of what is currently happening and of what it may be possible to achieve. To be critical does not mean fearlessly confronting underperforming teachers or boldly informing the cleaners that the classrooms are dirty! To be critical is to be restless, not a restlessness born from frustration or anger but born from a commitment to improve, develop and learn. It is important for you as head to have the sense of being a learner, as it brings with it a degree of humility which is a fundamental characteristic of successful leadership. Being critical also implies being open, open to ideas, suggestions from both within and without the school, together with a preparedness to engage with arguments.

If, as a headteacher, you are to be transformative, you will also need to apply particular skills with some care. The skills of advocacy will be essential if you are actually to change the way people think about something, and it is this deep-rooted change in people's thinking which is the most difficult to achieve. As a headteacher, changing the ways things are done may be simple or straightforward, but changing the way people might think is much more problematical. It requires patience and understanding about how others may make sense of new situations, or, indeed, see old established situations differently. We also know that the real agenda is not simply to change one aspect of schooling, but to change the way the school thinks about change. As a headteacher, therefore, you need to take the long view, although this has been increasingly difficult over the past few years. Taking the long view implies two things: you need to appreciate that it takes time to change and you need to understand that what needs changing may be the way the school views and handles change – the school culture. If your leadership is to transform, then again you must engage with staff in discussion and argument, and bring to those discussions the added dimensions of experience, knowledge and understanding. You must also provide a degree of wisdom. Leadership must know when to confront and challenge as well as when to withdraw. You must be sensitive to the mode of engagement and the nature of support so that you are aware when it is right to provide space, time, money or resources. As a headteacher you should seek to model through your behaviour the process of transformation. It may be a salutary experience for a headteacher to pause periodically, particularly when confronting a specific issue, and to consider how long it has taken you to arrive at your particular level of understanding. How much experiential baggage has contributed to your particular point of view? How many headteachers have you worked for? In how many schools? And how realistic is it to expect teachers to arrive at the same conclusions within a matter of days or weeks?

The suggestion that headteachers should be educators is not particularly astounding, yet how often do headteachers see themselves as educators of teachers or support staff? There are several powerful and compelling images which we could employ to describe being a headteacher, such as shepherd, parent, manager. One that may not spring immediately to mind in relation to staff is teacher. If your headship is to be educative then it must have some regard to an approach to staff development which is concerned to develop within each teacher the four elements of leadership. As a headteacher, you have an important and direct responsibility to educate the next generation of headteachers and to secure a future through teachers who also have a fundamental regard for educational values. This again emphasizes the importance of process within headship rather than simply outcomes. To be educative, leadership must allow for and provide all those things with which a class teacher is concerned. As the headteacher you must be concerned with providing appropriate learning opportunities for staff, interacting with them in a manner which promotes exploration and discovery, reminding them of what they know and can do, clarifying and challenging their thinking and making connections between different experiences. One must allow mistakes but give responsibility within a framework of expectations.

If your leadership is to be ethical then it must be able to demonstrate a commitment to the process of management not simply on the basis of how to get the job done, but from a commitment to democratic values and the consequent ways in which people should be treated.

These are major responsibilities which rest upon headteachers' shoulders and they demand courage, determination and humanity, but offer significant and worthwhile rewards. At the heart of this process is the concept of the learning school, first articulated by Holly and Southworth (1989) in which they are clear that a school must put the priorities of learning before the 'demands of the organisation'. They identify the key concepts for the learning school as:

- interactive and negotiative;
- creative and problem-solving;
- proactive and responsive;
- participative and collaborative;
- flexible and challenging;
- risk taking and enterprising;
- evaluative and reflective;
- supportive and developmental.

The attitudes, values and implied behaviour inherent within these key concepts stand in stark contrast to the current plethora of headteachers' job descriptions. Like many job descriptions, that of the headteacher does not always represent reality, and often has either a dreamlike or nightmarish quality depending on your point of view or perhaps the type of day you have had! The move towards creating job descriptions in schools was based upon a growing cynicism among managers and teachers. On the one hand, managers were being urged to pin teachers down by creating job descriptions which were as precise as possible about the responsibilities of individual teachers, a view based on the premise that many teachers were not pulling their weight. On the other hand, teachers also welcomed job descriptions but for very different reasons. They saw job descriptions as a form of protection against unreasonable demands and an ever-increasing workload. What is apparent is that job descriptions emerged from a state of mutual mistrust. As we pointed out earlier, the job description is a key document in the appraisal process, so it is ultimately a document deeply bound up with administrative surveillance.

If we accept the social nature of leadership in the sense that leaders need followers and leadership can be exercised by a variety of people, then it would seem reasonable to consult and negotiate about the nature of leadership. This can be a bold but liberating experience. Its boldness lies in the fact that as a headteacher you are rejecting the notion that it is through being the headteacher that you gain authority. You are 'letting go' and genuinely sharing the idea of leadership.

It is liberating, as it allows you a sense of freedom together with security, since you are much more aware of the expectations of others. It will also serve as a useful model for others to follow as they begin to exercise leadership themselves. So one way of defining the responsibilities of the headteacher is to ask others what they are looking for in a headteacher. Following the establishment of the vision, or indeed as part of the visioning process itself, a headteacher can challenge staff to articulate what they see as the headteacher's responsibilities. This need not be one-way traffic. You can argue and similarly challenge views with which you disagree and what this will begin to demonstrate is an openness and commitment to respond to the needs of others. What will inevitably emerge initially will be a messy, complex picture of expectations, but gradually these can be refined through further focused discussion. For instance, the perceptions of the headteacher's responsibility from the deputy's point of view will be very different from those of the newly qualified teacher or the recently promoted postholder. In each case, they will articulate specific demands to which a headteacher can respond at a variety of levels.

An approach such as this communicates many messages, the most important of which is the headteacher's preparedness to uphold the values of democratic schooling. It models many of the key concepts of the learning school and provides a very secure basis on which to build the most productive kinds of relationships. A fundamental belief underlying this approach is that there is very little distinction between the working relationships which are conducive to children's learning and those which produce schools to which staff feel enormous commitment.

Most, if not all, schools have common elements, headteachers and teachers. It is therefore entirely proper that it is these two roles which need the greatest clarity. It is also important, however, that they are defined in relation to each other. If we return to the notions of rights and responsibilities discussed in the previous chapter, we can see how inextricably linked these two jobs are. In a way, in defining responsibilities we are simultaneously defining rights. If staff are involved in identifying a headteacher's responsibilities, they are also defining a headteacher's rights and unavoidably articulating their own rights and responsibilities. We are involved here in defining the framework of expectations within which the working relationships occur. What entitlements do staff have and what obligations are they under?

It would seem appropriate at this stage to try to pin down entitlement and obligation by addressing some of the important tasks with which schools engage. Headteachers will, of course, have responsibilities in all of these tasks, but in a sense they are defined by everyone else's responsibilities. The key tasks are:

◆ classroom teaching;
◆ provision of a curriculum framework, including arrangements for assessment, and monitoring and evaluating;
◆ provision for special educational needs;
◆ provision for staff development.

It seems to us that these fundamental tasks share two features. First, they involve everyone in the school to some extent; second, they are sufficiently definable to require distinct organization and management. By looking at each of these tasks in turn we can begin to explore how they may relate to the responsibilities and rights of the various members of staff, including deputy headteachers, curriculum coordinators, classroom teachers and teaching support staff. Through this process, we can also define the headteacher's responsibilities in relation to each of these tasks. Inevitably what will be offered here is not a blueprint. All schools are different and size, together with financial circumstances, will play a part in any decisions that are made. What we are able to offer is a framework of rights and responsibilities based firmly on a clearly defined set of values and aspirations.

CLASSROOM TEACHING

In the majority of primary schools, most teachers will have a full-time teaching commitment. In larger schools deputies will perhaps not have direct responsibility for a class, but still have a significant teaching commitment, and headteachers may be in a similar position. In many small schools, headteachers will have responsibility for teaching a class of children. Given the fact that class teaching is the most fundamental job within schools and in addition is the activity with which most teachers are engaged for most of the time, it is remarkable how infrequently it is paid any real regard in books about primary school management. Since the task of classroom teaching is the most crucial, it would seem sensible to make that the first consideration in terms of articulating responsibilities.

All staff need to be involved in coming to a common understanding of what it means to be a classroom teacher at a particular school. This can be achieved in a variety of ways, depending upon the numbers involved. With only a small number of teachers it can be discussed at a series of staff meetings, but with larger numbers the process needs to be differently organized. One way is to ask two or three teachers, either individually or collectively, to prepare some ideas on paper to present to different groups of staff whose deliberations can eventually be put to the whole staff. It might be helpful to offer some guidance about the kinds of areas which will need to be addressed in terms of a class teacher's responsibility, which might include the following:

♦ preparedness to reflect upon the nature of teaching and learning;
♦ working with others, either teachers or teaching support staff;
♦ levels of engagement in curriculum planning and preparation;
♦ levels of engagement in decisions about whole-school policies;
♦ the responsibility class teachers should have for creating an appropriate learning environment.

These kinds of discussions can be extremely fruitful and provide valuable areas for further debate. The collaboration among staff in defining their responsibilities as class teachers offers both a clear statement of priorities and a model of operating. The difficulties (as always) will emerge in the detail and it may be impossible to agree on some areas. This does not diminish the impact and it is important to bear in mind that this process should not be over-concerned with defining any aspect in too much detail, as this can inhibit further discussion. As the responsibilities of the class teacher emerge, so will the parallel rights which in turn impact upon the responsibilities of others.

The importance of reaching broad agreements about what it means to be a class teacher at a particular school cannot be over-stressed. It is only when this is accomplished that the other key tasks which concern a school can begin to be tackled. It is from the classroom teaching that all else flows. The other key tasks and the nature of responsibilities accorded to the tasks are fundamentally about supporting the work of class teaching. In other words, once the meaning of class teaching is articulated, other rights and responsibilities can begin to be unpacked. Because this is a complex business, as we start to identify the other responsibilities so, in effect, do we put more detail upon aspects of class teaching. For example, as a school considers how it creates a curriculum framework, so it will begin to identify what part the class teacher plays in planning, assessment and defining responsibilities within the field of special educational needs. Through examination of the various rights and responsibilities, possible structures and systems of meetings will suggest themselves. In this way, activities will begin to take on an holistic perspective and responsibilities should begin to become interdependent. Before we move on to other tasks, however, it is important that we consider carefully what might be the rights available to a class teacher. Essentially those rights, or what we may refer to as entitlements, would be very closely bound up with the other key tasks since, as we have said, these should be essentially aimed at supporting the work of class teaching. The rights of a class teacher, therefore, reflect and confirm the importance of the other tasks and would be concerned with:

◆ the right to be provided with a clear curriculum framework within which to place his or her own work and the right to have an input into that framework;
◆ the right to be consulted and informed about whole-school issues;
◆ the right to a programme of staff development which provides opportunities for further learning and offers a framework of support in day-to-day activities.

As we can see, what is being created is a series of intertwining and interlocking rights and responsibilities which together begin to realize the vision of the working relationships among staff. At this point we can begin to look at the responsibilities which are concerned with creating a whole-school curriculum framework.

PROVISION OF A CURRICULUM FRAMEWORK

Before we explore the responsibilities which go with this it is perhaps important to define what we mean by 'curriculum framework'. For the purposes of this book a curriculum framework is taken to mean those elements which are agreed by the staff to provide the reference points for their own curriculum planning. In other words, it is a collective way of describing the various subject schemes of work and the whole-school policies which make a direct impact upon the curriculum, such as assessment, equal opportunities and teaching and learning styles.

To explore the provision of a curriculum framework is to confront directly the issues surrounding curriculum leadership. Curriculum leadership is a vital component in any school and is increasingly recognized as an aspect of schools which has the potential to be developed further. Curriculum leadership operates on at least two distinct levels. At one level we can assume that there is an overall curriculum coordinator who has a responsibility to support the work of curriculum subject coordinators, who form a second level. Again, depending upon the size and nature of the school, the organization of this will vary. For example, it can often be split between Key Stages in larger schools, where there may also be coordinators responsible for assessment across the curriculum. Having said this, curriculum coordination across the school is a major task and should be the responsibility of either the headteacher or the deputy headteacher. This assertion is in part a direct result of the perceived lack of involvement of headteachers, in particular in curriculum management. The initiatives which have eaten into headteachers' time have ironically taken them away from the curriculum. This issue was addressed in direct terms by the 'Three Wise Men's' report, in which it was said:

> There are two broad approaches to primary headship. On the one hand, the emphasis is on the head as administrator; on the other, the emphasis is squarely on the need to provide educational leadership. There is a view at present in England that the introduction of LMS means that the primary head must become an administrator or chief executive. We reject this view absolutely . . . Primary Schools exist to provide a curriculum which fosters the development of their pupils. Headteachers must take the leading role in ensuring the quality of curricular provision and they cannot do this without involving themselves directly and centrally in the planning, transactions and evaluations of the curriculum.
>
> (DES 1992)

This view is one which we wholeheartedly endorse. A primary responsibility of headship is the responsibility for the curriculum. Having said that, however, it is inevitably a responsibility which has to be shared and delegated, and in reality the curriculum is coordinated through a number of teachers who have rights and responsibilities extra to those which are directly concerned with their class teaching. The responsibilities, as usual, take on two forms, those concerned with tasks and those concerned with process. It is the latter which are the more important. Subject coordinators are key players in the school. It is vital that they share the school's values and are in tune with the nature of the working relationships. It is they who will have the major responsibility to create and maintain the vision of working relationships which becomes a reality, and it is for them to model the process involved in school development. The responsibilities of the subject coordinator are fundamental to the school and to colleagues, not merely to the task in hand.

The job of curriculum coordinator has been particularly high-lighted since the introduction of the National Curriculum. They were seen as instrumental in the introduction of the various National Curriculum subjects into schools, and what they actually did has become the object of various pieces of research (see Webb and Vulliamy 1996). The story of curriculum coordinators is not an unfamiliar one. The nature of curriculum responsibility and how to manage it have been subjected to as much training as being a headteacher. Courses which explore the management of change, working with others and developing management skills abound, all providing similar messages. The demands on coordinators have also changed. Initially they were mainly concerned with supporting colleagues through the introduction of resources, ideas and activities into school. Some coordinators gave gentle professional advice focused upon their particular subject. Many coordinators have made a significant impact upon the success of a school but the demands have now developed further, to the extent that coordinators produce action plans for inclusion in school development plans, manage budgets and often work in classrooms alongside colleagues. As the baton of 'quality assurance' has been taken up by the managerialists, so curriculum coordinators are now being urged to get into the business of monitoring and evaluating, thus becoming the school's internal subject inspectors. For the vast majority of primary teachers, this is on top of a full-time teaching commitment!

There would be very little disagreement among teachers and heads about the tasks which confront the curriculum coordinator, although lively discussions could be had about the areas of emphasis. It is crucially important, however, to bear in mind the vision of the relationships which will determine the process through which these tasks are undertaken. Day *et al.* (1993) provide a thoroughly useful analysis of much of this process and explore curriculum leadership in some detail. Our purpose in this instance is to provide a broad outline of the responsibilities and rights inherent within the tasks. The major responsibility of curriculum coordinators is to be committed to the agreed vision of school life and to have an acute awareness of what this means in everyday activity. They have a responsibility to model the process of school improvement through reflection and collaboration. It is this fundamental responsibility which again exposes the inadequacy of many job descriptions, since it is an intangible component. In terms of subject-related tasks there would seem to be three major responsibilities which, taken together provide the kind of support which we would argue is the right or entitlement of every class teacher. Those responsibilities are to provide:

♦ a framework of operations;
♦ a framework of support;
♦ a framework for evaluation.

It is worth having a brief look at what each of these might include.

By a framework of operations we refer to that part of the curriculum framework which consists of schemes of work and any subject policies or guidelines. Essentially this framework is providing the parameters within which class teachers or year groups set their own curriculum planning. Once this is established it needs to be enhanced by the next framework.

A framework of support is simply that part of the job which is involved in maintaining up-to-date knowledge about developments in the subject, ensuring that resources are available and that any new ideas and activities concerned with the subject are brought to the attention of all staff.

The framework for evaluation is the final subject-related task which is currently the priority for many schools. It is this area which has been most recently highlighted, and schools feel an acute need for coordinators to play their part in accounting for the standards attained within their subjects. The need to monitor and evaluate has been stressed to schools, particularly through the activities of Ofsted. There is a temptation on the part of schools to copy the Ofsted model of inspection and to set up systems which tend to portray curriculum coordinators as internal inspectors. This tendency may develop further as more headteachers become involved in Ofsted inspections themselves. A headteacher needs to consider carefully how the school evaluates itself and maintain a very clear distinction between its own internal mechanisms and those of Ofsted. Any degree of reflection about what is achieved clearly implies an element of evaluation. If curriculum leadership is to be critical, there has to be that sense of restlessness about current practice and achievement. This restlessness is based not upon apprehension of impending inspection, but a determination to do the best possible job. Any evaluation undertaken by coordinators must be done with teachers, rather than to them, and should demonstrate and eventually implant the process of evaluation within each teacher. In other words, the responsibility of the coordinator is to support each teacher in his or her own reflection upon the activities of a particular class. This may well involve some of the practices used by Ofsted, such as looking carefully at children's work, but this should be done in collaboration with teacher colleagues rather than in isolation. It could also include developing school portfolios and good recording systems which track children's progress. Much has been written about working alongside colleagues as a way and a means of monitoring the curriculum and it is worth just considering this for a moment. In reality the opportunities which will be available for this to occur in the average primary school will be extremely limited. It is our view that such a strategy is not particularly helpful in monitoring the curriculum simply because of the infrequency of the activity, but it can, and often does, become a strategy to support colleagues through teaching partnerships. It certainly has a part to play in staff development.

What is important within these responsibilities is the realization that the activities of curriculum coordinators should make a positive impact upon what happens in classrooms and particularly on what children are able to achieve. This refocusing of the job has been a welcome development in recent years, as assessing children's achievement often did not feature in a coordinator's agenda. As always, with responsibilities come rights. Once again, a headteacher's responsibilities are closely bound up with the rights of others. If curriculum coordinators are to have the ability to fulfil their responsibilities, then they have particular rights. These will reflect the overall pattern of relationships within the school, but could include the following.

- Receiving support without interference.
- Being able to make mistakes. This is important in any educational enterprise, but if we want teachers to grow and develop then mistakes are an inevitable consequence of taking risks.
- Having access to the headteacher and support networks outside the school.
- Being given the opportunity to do the job. This does need a degree of planning and it is important that time is managed carefully. Rather than all coordinators having the right to the same time, the school may have particular priorities which means that time to do jobs is not distributed equally, but reflects the priorities.

What is offered here is a broad view of the rights and responsibilities of a curriculum leader. The detail (if that is what is required) can be agreed among the staff in the same way that the headteacher's rights and responsibilities were made explicit. What is certainly the case is that there are no blueprints for the job, since it will be different from school to school. What is vital is that the rights and responsibilities sit comfortably within the school's vision of its working relationships.

PROVISION FOR SPECIAL EDUCATIONAL
NEEDS

This is identified on the third key internal task, as it touches almost every school activity. It also carries with it quite specific responsibilities which it is important to make explicit. Having said that, some of the responsibilities of the special needs coordinator (SENCO) will be implicit within those applicable to the curriculum coordinator, and the process or climate in which the work is done will be similar. The specific responsibilities of the SENCO include:

- ensuring that the requirements of the Code of Practice for Special Educational Needs are fully met (this has clear implications for the maintenance of records, the updating and monitoring of individual educational plans, the annual reviews and ensuring that the school fulfils the requirements of any statements);
- coordinating the work of special needs support assistants;
- coordinating the involvement of parents;
- coordinating the involvement of outside agencies.

It is beyond the capacity of this book to explore the detailed responsibilities of the SENCO, but it is worth bearing in mind that a school's values could legitimately be identified through its approach to special needs. It is through a school's commitment (or not) to making provision for special needs that it will express its vision of the nature of education. The approach taken to special needs is a powerful indicator of the nature and purpose of the school as a whole.

The SENCO, of course, enjoys the same rights as everyone else, but there is another specific right which should be clearly articulated. The SENCO should have very clear expectations about the precise responsibilities of the class teacher in providing for special needs. As a school makes provision for special needs, and particularly as provision is extended, there may be a temptation for class teachers to 'pass the buck' for special needs to the SENCO. This particular SENCO's 'right' could be specifically articulated within the responsibilities of the class teachers. Once again, what we see is that the way the school operates is a complex intertwining of various rights and responsibilities. We can now turn to the final area of school activity which is crucial to the nature of working relationships.

STAFF DEVELOPMENT

This is a fundamental issue because it is directly concerned with the nature of education. It is about the continuing education and development of all staff within the school and, like special needs, is a feature of school life which can act as a window through which we can begin to see the underlying values and attitudes which guide the school. It is also a symptom of the school's culture. We have already made clear that involving staff in a continuous striving to improve by providing opportunities to reflect upon and refine their practice is a major responsibility of educational leadership. To discuss the nature of staff development is to go to the heart of the school's working relationships. Whoever takes on this major responsibility must be cognizant of the possibilities which staff development creates and should appreciate the central importance of staff development to the well-being of the school. Too often, staff development coordinators are left to administer a budget and book courses, rather than engaging directly in promoting improvement through reflection. Schools are becoming increasingly sophisticated in identifying their own requirements and are also much better at seeing how they can unlock the resources they already have to tackle new initiatives. Consultants, advisors or support from outside, while being important, can only assist a school to improve itself. In a very real sense, staff development coordinators have a pivotal responsibility for one of the fundamental purposes of the school: the improvement of teaching. These responsibilities are difficult to pin down in terms of tasks, as they are bound up with ideas and attitudes dependent upon those leadership elements discussed earlier. In this sense they have a responsibility 'to be' as much as 'to do'. Such responsibilities would incorporate:

◆ understanding that staff development is a continuous and intrinsic part of the job of teaching;
◆ having knowledge and understanding about learning;
◆ appreciating the importance and potential of teachers working reflectively in partnerships;
◆ maintaining various networks within and outside the school;
◆ understanding that all initiatives have staff development implications.

This is only to touch the surface of what it means to coordinate staff development. The qualities it requires are, in many respects, already contained within the characteristics of the learning school. As before, the rights of the coordinator are bound up with the responsibilities of others. He or she has the right to expect some degree of involvement on the part of staff and the right to appropriate support from the headteacher.

The staff development coordinator also has the right to expect that all staff are working within a culture which is amenable to staff development, while at the same time contributing to the creation of that culture. This is another complex, chicken and egg situation. In exploring staff development, there needs to be an appreciation that we are dealing with both the formal and informal. Staff development occurs as much informally as it does formally, and therefore everyone bears some responsibility to ensure that it is an intrinsic part of school life. This means that planning meetings, year meetings and staff meetings all constitute opportunities for staff development. Those with specific responsibilities must be conscious that they will model modes of behaviour which in themselves will set examples for younger teachers.

This brings us to the end of those key tasks which each school needs to accomplish. We have explored the rights and responsibilities of various members of staff who may be engaged directly or indirectly in accomplishing the key tasks and so we have inevitably looked at class teachers, curriculum coordinators and SENCOs. The omission in this section so far has been the deputy headteacher. The role of the deputy headteacher creates a complex problem. On the one hand he or she is identified as a key member of staff who has a significant influence on the success or otherwise of the school (Mortimore *et al.* 1988) but has no clearly identified universal responsibilities unless we regard deputizing for the headteacher as a generic responsibility. This is in contrast to the more specific responsibilities identified for curriculum coordinators. The fact that the deputy head's job is relatively undefined is both a strength and weakness. On balance, and perhaps unsurprisingly, we consider it a strength, as it provides yet more opportunity for a school to respond to its own particular circumstances. The deputy's job clearly needs to encompass some of those key tasks and so his or her responsibilities and rights will be defined through them. It is worth giving some consideration to which of the tasks a deputy should engage with in a direct way. In terms of curriculum leadership, he or she can often play a major part in developing and supporting a core subject. In terms of broader leadership he or she could take on the job of SENCO or coordinating staff development. In some respects, both the latter options provide opportunities for a wider and deeper engagement with children and staff. Webb and Vulliamy (1996) see the potential significance of staff development with regard to the deputy headteacher. 'While responsibility for staff professional development and INSET was generally undefined and underdeveloped, it is a potentially important and demanding role.' Others have argued that the deputy should become the curriculum supremo, with a title such as 'director of curricular studies' (Harrison and Gill 1992). What does seem both important and appropriate is that the deputy head has a significant job which involves a whole-school dimension and it is this dimension which is critical.

The relationship between the headteacher and deputy is obviously a crucial one. It is vital that the deputy has a whole-school job so that he or she is able to demonstrate and model the school vision across the whole school. At the same time, the relationship with the head must also represent in microcosm the nature of relationships at all levels. This calls for genuine partnership and collaboration which is focused upon shared values and attitudes. Nias *et al.* (1989) argued that the deputy was 'the leading culture bearer' securing staff commitment to the school's 'mission' through his or her actions and examples. In other words, a deputy has a powerful impact upon the cultural circumstances of the school. What this means is that the deputy has a responsibility to promote and sustain those processes which flow directly from the vision of the school's working relationships, and the particular relationship with the head should embody the qualities and practices to sustain the vision. A further responsibility is to develop and maintain relationships with all staff which also reflect the emphasis upon collaboration.

Before we leave the subject of working relationships it is worth giving some thought to the kinds of structures needed to support these. Any staffing structures must reflect the nature of the relationships but once again it can become a complex issue of chicken and egg – some relationships can be a reflection of the structure. To a large extent, structures will be dictated by circumstances. It is of very little use talking about senior management teams if there are only three or four teachers in a school. In fact there is a good case to be made that the concept of a senior management team is not appropriate for a primary school, as it emphasizes a hierarchy without focusing upon the jobs to be done. It is also emphasizing a degree of exclusivity which would not sit comfortably with the relationships described here. The emphasis within any structure should be embracing rather than excluding, it should be task-oriented rather than hierarchical and it should reflect an implicit understanding that all developments and activities contribute to defining and maintaining the school's culture. All tasks have a part to play in staff development insofar as they provide different staff with new opportunities. It seems to us that any structures need a large measure of flexibility and that they should assume and support varying degrees of collaboration. This may mean that curriculum coordinators work through a curriculum subject team, it may mean establishing teaching partnerships using the notion of the 'critical friend' and it could mean working parties being established to get a job done and then being disbanded when the task is complete. Such structures would provide opportunities for leadership to be exercised by several members of staff, as they would tap into a variety of expertise and allow everyone to have access to models of collaboration.

An increasingly important element in school life is the growing number of people employed to support teachers. These members of staff are either assigned to particular children with special needs or brought in to work alongside classroom teachers. It is important that classroom assistants are included within any school's vision and are enabled to make a full contribution to the work of the school. In the past, schools were often rather ambivalent about classroom assistants and other support staff, sometimes to the extent that assistants were not always welcome in staffrooms. As their number increases and the impact that they make becomes increasingly apparent, they too must become an integral part of the pattern of relationships. This also implies particular rights and responsibilities. We have already touched upon some of the rights which may be carried by support staff, which would certainly include:

♦ to be regarded as colleagues who have a full part to play in school;
♦ to be included in discussion about whole-school issues and in particular to be consulted about aspects which impact upon their specific areas;
♦ to have access to staff development opportunities;
♦ to have some input into the planning and assessing of curriculum provision.

As they work in classrooms these rights will become more specific, but it is a responsibility of the class teacher to involve the assistant fully in what is happening. It is the class teacher who can enable (or not) children to gain from the work of the assistant. This involves class teachers spending time explaining the learning intentions behind activities and providing guidance to assistants about what strategies could be used by them to achieve the intention. If this professional dialogue is missing, then assistants will not be in a position to think and reflect upon their work and there is a possibility that children will not gain from an activity. It is this close professional discussion which seems to us to be at the heart of ensuring that classroom support is used in the best way. Once again, as the headteacher, you will need to be very active in promoting and modelling this collaborative way of working.

The final part of this chapter exploring working relationships will look at that between the headteacher and governing body, in particular upon the relationship with the chair of governors. It is a truism that governors play an increasingly important part in managing schools. As their responsibilities have been increased and defined so their involvement has become more vital. It has become such an issue that it is not unusual to come across the notion of 'managing governing bodies' as part of a training course for headteachers. For us, this has a rather sinister connotation and could be taken to imply, at worst, a degree of manipulation, or at best, how to deal with a necessary evil. Perhaps this is too pessimistic. There is plenty of anecdotal evidence from headteachers that when the relationship between head and chair of governors is a good one it makes a great difference to the job of being a headteacher. There is also plenty of evidence which suggests that when the relationship turns sour it is very damaging for the school.

Our starting point must be the vision itself. If governors are to subscribe to the vision and feel a sense of commitment to it, then they should be involved in defining it. They need some input to the school process which explores the nature of education, the kind of working relationships and the nature of the school curriculum to which the school aspires. In some respects, forging a shared vision among governors may present some difficulties. Teachers at least share the common experience of teaching, but governors can represent a very diverse range of experiences. The governing body could potentially be made up of people with widely differing views, attitudes and values based largely upon their own everyday experiences. Having said that, governors are (or should be) united in a single purpose – namely the success of the school. Involving them in the visioning process is important since it can be helpful in providing opportunities for governors to work with teachers and other members of staff, but perhaps more importantly because it gives the governors a greater insight into the context within which they, along with staff, are working. This can have enormous benefits when governors are confronted with different issues to do with their particular responsibilities. For instance, they will be in a much stronger position to exercise their responsibilities for special needs provision if they know, understand and share the school's vision of how it promotes achievement for children with difficulties. Governors will be much better placed to make decisions about curriculum provision if they know, understand and share the vision of teaching and learning. It is commonplace advice offered to governors (for example, the Advisory Centre for Education (ACE) 1995) that they should regularly discuss values and attitudes as a governing body, but that they should also engage in such discussion with all staff.

The critical relationship is that between the headteacher and chair of governors. The potential for disharmony is considerable, mainly because there are significant grey areas in the statutory responsibilities of governing bodies and headteachers. Most disagreements occur when boundaries are thought to have been breached. The simplest way of preventing such problems is to have clearly defined responsibilities and tasks. How they are defined and allocated is not too important, it is awareness of them that is critical. It is our view that the significant responsibility is upon the headteachers to make the relationship work. As the Advisory Centre for Education advises, 'As far as heads are concerned, it would transform relationships if they could see the effective development of a Governing Body as a professional challenge worthy of the most outstanding talent' (ACE 1995). It may be, in fairness, to this that the idea of 'managing the governing body' refers. What is clearly the case is that headteachers need to understand that governors will require time and attention. It is only the foolhardy headteacher who contemplates significant developments without consulting governors. If the pattern of the relationship is one of regular meetings, mutual consultation and a degree of flexibility about who does what, then there should be few problems. The governing body should be operating at a strategic level, not on the day-to-day organization of the school. Governors do need to be consulted, however, on anything which may cause some concern to parents or provoke dissension among staff. This might include changing the organization of year groups, altering approaches to teaching reading or developing new whole-school policies.

We have said that problems can arise when boundaries are breached – often headteachers feel that governors have encroached on their territory and sense that the governors are interfering. In some cases the problem is the exact opposite, with governing bodies reluctant to take on some of their new responsibilities. This is sometimes the case where governing bodies are well established and have found it hard to adjust to the new demands. Again the onus is upon the headteacher to begin to develop the governing body and bring it more on to centre stage. One way of achieving this is to concentrate on tasks rather than attitudes. It is easier, as we acknowledged earlier, to change what people do rather than what they think, and it is also the case that as they change what they do they may come to think differently. What this might mean is that headteachers begin to specify jobs that need to be done and ask the governing body actually to do them. This could take the form of collecting ideas, writing reports, dealing with the administration of a particular problem or liaising with a member of staff over policy development. As they work with each other and members of staff they will be initiated into the processes which lie at the heart of the school. Alongside this gradual introduction it is also important that governors have full access to a programme of training, which will not only explain their responsibilities but give them some ideas about how to fulfil them.

This chapter has been continually concerned with the nature of working relationships at all levels. The primary responsibility for creating successful relationships rests upon you as headteacher but they rely upon everyone to sustain them. What is being proposed here is both simple and complex. It is simple in the sense that the nature of the relationships is fundamental to the success of the school, they are at the heart of the enterprise and touch all aspects of schooling. It is complex because people are complex and relationships are never entirely smooth or predictable. What is being asked of headteachers is also demanding and difficult, and will require enormous skill, understanding, determination and, perhaps above all, confidence. As a headteacher you will need the confidence to maintain a healthy scepticism about current managerial shibboleths, the confidence to go with what you know – that the nature of the job is often messy and unpredictable. You will also need confidence to let go, to relinquish power and push it towards others, to allow others to lead – all this despite the urge to control. Finally, you will need the confidence to act in the knowledge that what you are doing takes time. Remember how long it has taken you personally to arrive at what you think today – can you really expect other people to arrive at similar conclusions within a matter of days?

7

WORKING WITH
PARENTS AND THE
COMMUNITY

Deciding upon what kind of part, if any, a school is to play within its local community is an important element within the school's vision. For most primary schools the community is predominantly, but not exclusively, parents, and so the relationship that a school establishes with its parent body is an important dimension of the school's activity. In earlier chapters we discussed some of the dilemmas facing parents and schools. There is some evidence (Hughes *et al.* 1990) that these dilemmas are more theoretical than real. One theoretical dilemma is the tension between seeing parents as consumers or as partners. As consumers they are in receipt of a service which is provided for them by schools, but if they are partners then they are deeply implicated in the service they are receiving. As we have noted, this dilemma may be exaggerated. Despite the encouragement of government, parents do not particularly see themselves as consumers of education and they do not see education as a commodity to be purchased. Most parents, when asked if they thought of themselves as consumers (see Hughes *et al.* 1990), were in fact rather puzzled by the notion. Although parents, again theoretically, are aware that they have some choice about which school to send their child to, most parents of primary school children choose their local school. For many parents the notion of a choice is a spurious one, since the next nearest school may be several miles away. Despite all the publicity about the apparent weaknesses of primary education the majority of parents of primary aged children are satisfied with the school of their choice. Having acknowledged this, however, does not mean that everything in the garden is rosy. There is considerable rhetoric about parental involvement, partnerships and open door policies which, when looked at in detail, do little to enable parents to make a significant contribution to school life or to assist their children's learning. Research by the National Foundation for Educational Research (NFER: Jowett *et al.* 1991) has highlighted some of the limitations inherent within the rhetoric.

> The use of the word 'involvement' for a range of . . . activities has served to obscure the key issues. School may have a great many parents providing assistance and see this as a thriving system of parental involvement, whereas very little dialogue or learning by either parents or staff may be taking place.

In the same way that working relationships within a school must go beyond the superficial notion of getting on, so must the working relationships between a school and its parent community go beyond simplistic levels of involvement which fail to engage parents in either their children's learning or the way in which the school operates. If the school's central and fundamental concern is learning, then parents must be involved not only in their own children's learning but as learners themselves. This is to propose a relationship which is very different from the one envisaged by the 'parents as consumers' relationship, which in some schools has been seen as threatening and has led to the emergence of marketing as one of their current concerns.

Parental involvement is an area of school life which is both demanding and difficult. The potential for misunderstanding is considerable and it would be unrealistic not to acknowledge the potential for conflict. As with governors, parents represent a broad spectrum of humanity and different parents will have different views of how schools should operate and what they should teach. Again, however, at primary school level it would be very easy to exaggerate the differences and not recognize the similarities. The overwhelming majority of parents (see Hughes *et al.* 1990) who were asked what they considered to be the most important feature of school replied that it was that their children be happy and that the ethos of relationships at all levels should be positive. In other words, primary schools start with a great advantage, in that most parents want to approve of and support their local school. The question for schools, and particularly you as the headteacher, is how to develop that positive start to achieve the kind of relationship which is fruitful and productive.

There can be no blueprint for how a school relates to its parents, since it will depend upon the nature of the school and the social circumstances within which it functions. Having said that, there are some guiding principles which most schools could share. Since this area can be difficult, it may be helpful in the early stages, when the relationships are growing, to limit the aims of what you want to achieve and to target particular groups of parents. Before any of this is tackled, however, there is one fundamental state of affairs which should exist, namely that the school itself has an agreed and shared vision of how it wants to relate to its parents. It is very frustrating and confusing for parents if there is a lack of consistency about how they are received and dealt with by different members of staff. For instance, if the school decides to have an 'open-door' policy there is a need to agree exactly what that means, not only in terms of what happens, but also in terms of people's attitudes and behaviour. It is counterproductive to suggest that teachers are always available if the availability comes with a thinly disguised resentment at having to arrive at school early or remain behind at the end of the day. It is essentially attitudes which will dictate the nature of the relationship.

Establishing appropriate relationships is not easy. It again calls for considerable nerve and confidence on your part, since ultimately it may require a degree of power-sharing, or at least allowing power to pass down the line. If the notion of power-sharing is not part of the agenda, this raises questions such as: what is the nature of the partnership, on whose terms is the partnership being established and how can it be a partnership of equals? If the rhetoric of partnership is to become a reality then it is the responsibility of the school to initiate the development, and make positive moves to embrace the parental community. What is clearly the case is that schools which do seek a genuine partnership with their parents are generally more successful in providing an appropriate education for their pupils (see Mortimore *et al.* 1988). This view of parental involvement was explored by the Community Education Development Centre (CEDC 1993), which suggested that if a genuine partnership was being sought it would take time to develop, but would include the following:

- the sharing of power, responsibility and ownership;
- a degree of accountability;
- shared aims and goals;
- joint action.

Each of these aspects is challenging. In offering to share power and responsibility, you would be inviting parents to share in the same process of learning and development engaged in by members of staff. You would be demonstrating that educative aspect of leadership which is concerned to establish and promote a culture of learning. You would be actively concerned to enable parents to exercise leadership within the framework established by the school. While this is the first aspect highlighted by the CEDC it is likely to be the last one to be achieved and it is only through working on the others that this one will be realized.

To achieve a 'degree of mutuality' schools must establish what the NFER (Jowett *et al.* 1991) refers to as 'a climate of real approachability and opportunities for dialogue'. This goes beyond setting up various meetings and involves careful consideration of the nature of the meetings, what is said, by whom and how it is said. Too often, schools and parents can be likened to America and Britain, people divided by a common language. Jowett *et al.* (1991) have demonstrated the limited and unproductive nature of many meetings held at schools for parents. At best, meetings pass off without incident, although many parents are none the wiser for attending, while at worst parents are made to feel uncomfortable or inadequate and therefore unlikely to return. To create the climate of real approachability, schools must seek dialogue rather than simply seeking to inform. It is important that the purposes of various meetings are clear, especially in deciding if they are to inform, consult or indeed decide upon a particular matter. One thing is certain: if schools decide to consult parents then they must be prepared to listen and respond to parents' views. This is not to say that schools do what parents want, but it is to acknowledge that they have views and opinions about what happens and they are entitled to have these taken into account when decisions are made. The acknowledgement of parents' views and the visible response on the part of the school will go a long way towards creating a climate of trust and openness.

Partnerships will work best when there is a set of shared aims, so you must work to achieve a common vision with parents. Again this is not easy. We have seen from previous research (Hughes *et al.* 1990) that parental aspirations are generally reasonable and unsurprising. They wish their children to be happy and they want them to succeed in acquiring a range of important skills. These are not a million miles away from the basic aspirations that primary schools will have for their pupils. Similarly, parents talk about the importance of the relationships and the contribution those make to successful schools. It would not be unreasonable to share the vision for the school with parents, and very possible to consult them about some aspects of the vision and so enable them to have an input into the future. There will be differences and in some cases conflicts. Inevitably teachers have equal concern for all children while parents ultimately have a concern for their own child. What is demonstrable in many schools is that these difficulties are not insurmountable, particularly if you remember that most parents of primary age children are very satisfied with what their children are being offered.

Partnerships do not suddenly appear. They develop and grow through people working, thinking and talking together. The idea of joint action is therefore important. It is through the doing that bonds are formed and mutual understandings worked out. The joint action can take many forms. It can be focused upon fund-raising, it can focus upon a curriculum issue, it can focus upon a particular area of school improvement. There are many and varied opportunities for involvement to lead to genuine partnership.

The key to successful partnerships between home and school is the quality of communication. This is a function of both attitude and language. We have already stressed the need to develop an attitude throughout the school which recognizes and welcomes the role of parents in educating their children. There are, however, occasions when the language used to communicate with parents can itself become a barrier to understanding. Writing or talking about educational issues without using jargon or 'teacherese' is a difficult skill – it is, however, a vitally important one for headteachers to acquire. The NFER research to which we referred above showed that on many occasions at the end of a meeting the perceptions of teachers and parents are quite different. Teachers may feel that a meeting was successful because it allowed them to get over a message, but parents can come away without any real understanding or raised awareness. Jowett *et al.* (1991) write that 'School policy was presented as an unalterable fact without explanation or discussion which sometimes left parents confused and with unanswered queries.' Some statements and assertions from headteachers can be very damaging: 'one mother explained "I've learned that I've been teaching Hugh wrong for four years, teaching him the wrong way to do his reading and all sorts. I've just been told its completely wrong. He's got to do it all over again".' What this points to is the need for schools to think about and look carefully at the words they use and ensure that they are words which do not exclude parents or make them feel inadequate. Written and spoken explanations need to be accessible to all parents, who also need to feel comfortable about requesting clarification where it is needed.

The role of headteachers in discussing parents' personal problems with them is not a new one. It is self-evident that if a family is experiencing some form of stress, owing to financial difficulties or because of marital breakdown, there is often some effect on children which may well be manifest in school. Children may become withdrawn or aggressive towards their peers or perhaps disaffected in the classroom. There may be no obvious signs that they are unsettled, but a parent may feel that the school should know about the change in family circumstances, and schools will, of course, encourage parents to inform them of any situation which may have some bearing on a child's behaviour or performance in school. The sharing of such information can often become an unburdening of the problem, and it is the head who is usually the 'listening ear' in these situations.

Webb and Vulliamy (1996) highlight your role as 'headteacher as social worker':

> we were surprised at the frequency with which headteachers, and by no means only those in socially deprived areas, were having to counsel parents about their, rather than the children's problems. It seems as if an unintended consequence of an open-door policy, which is widely advocated in the literature as home–school links, is that heads are increasingly having to adopt the role of a social worker.

The authors illustrate clearly the potential consequence of extending a genuine welcome to parents and establishing a climate of trust between home and school. In such situations and in an era of tremendous pressures on families created by factors such as unemployment, negative equity and an increasing divorce rate, it is hardly surprising that schools often provide the most obvious source of advice and counselling. At the time that these demands on a school appear to be rising, there is a decrease in the support networks available in other sectors of the education service. Education welfare officers are over-stretched or in some areas no longer exist, and few schools have access to a home–school liaison officer. Webb and Vulliamy (1996) demonstrate that the 'headteacher as a social worker' problem is generally overlooked in studies of the headteacher role.

> For many heads in our sample, interaction with parents, some of which took the form of counselling, represented the most time-consuming aspect of their role. And yet this aspect of a head's job appears to be totally ignored, not only in management manuals for headteachers (Harrison and Gill 1992) but also in OFSTED's handbook for the inspection of schools (1993) and in their discussion papers (1994).

If this dimension of your role is so critical, then you face some dilemmas. How much time can you afford to give to listening to or guiding individual parents, which inevitably detracts from your substantial responsibilities for the running of the school and the furthering of the quality of the experiences offered to all children? How far should you be a natural port of call for a parent with a problem, especially when you have worked to create an effective structure for parental involvement which invites such access, and when do you decide that the situation lies beyond your professional remit or expertise and others would be better placed to advise and support?

There are, of course, no straightforward answers to these questions. Each situation will be different and the very nature of the problems which parents will bring to the school means that decisions often have to be made spontaneously in the light of the prevailing circumstances. No headteacher will turn away a parent who is clearly distressed and anxious to talk. But what of the parent who arrives at regular intervals expecting to have immediate access to you to discuss the latest developments in a particular situation in some detail, or who has a need to cover the same ground repeatedly? These are not extremes and will be recognized by many headteachers as very real within their schools. There is a fine distinction between schools offering support to parents under stress and becoming an essential prop to those parents on a personal level.

Schools do need to create their own network of communications within the community. Although headteachers may be the first line of contact, there are a range of services available and schools can offer support to parents by knowing to whom else they can turn in social services, the health authority, volunteer organizations or religious communities. Although it may take some time, it may be well worth while to make personal contact with people working within such services or groups. Apart from an increased knowledge of what a particular organization may offer, it would be helpful to have an established link with individuals. Distressed parents are more likely to respond to a suggestion that they telephone a named person who might be able to help, rather than just the duty officer at the local social services office, for example. An initial telephone call from you alerting a particular organization to a need for some support for a family can provide a useful introduction for parents in a vulnerable position. If parents are making frequent demands on the school for advice, then it is an indication that they trust the school and that it is performing a valuable role. As well as responding to such requests, schools can be proactive in alerting parents to the range of services available locally. A list of local agencies or volunteer groups with some brief details about their functions can be displayed on a parents' noticeboard or available in a community room.

There are obviously more aspects to community involvement than using local services. As with parental involvement, links with the community can take a variety of forms and it is worth clarifying the purposes of the various levels of involvement. It is self-evident that a school is part of a community; in some situations it may be at the heart of it. The use made of school premises by a variety of groups, the school's use of local facilities or the location of a playgroup or after-school club on the school site will bring headteacher, staff and children into contact with a large group of people outside the parent body. Any community will have particular perspectives on its local school, which may be based on limited experience by some individuals and frequent contact by others. Parents are part of the community and will express views on the school; most prospective parents will have received a view of a school before crossing its threshold.

All headteachers would want that view to be a positive one. As we have discussed, research shows that generally it is (Hughes *et al.* 1991). That does not mean there is room for complacency; a dissatisfied parent or a refusal to provide a meeting place for the youth club (both of which may be unavoidable for very practical reasons) will create negative feelings which can go beyond the school gate. There is little that can be done to militate against this happening in any school from time to time, but schools will want to consider how they can maintain a positive profile within the community. Apart from the marketing aspect in considering the school's image, no school will ignore the potential for making use of the community to enrich the curriculum offered to the children. As with so many aspects of what you do as headteacher, it is a question of balance; supporting community activities, use of the locality and involvement of local people in school life can have very positive benefits, but if such involvement begins to become so time consuming that it detracts from the main purposes of the school then it is time for a reappraisal.

SUMMARY

We began this book by highlighting the paradox of headship. The paradox is that as headteachers you have been given an increasing degree of autonomy in many aspects of your job, but your ability to influence the curriculum and assessment arrangements is increasingly prescribed. As headteachers have been given power so their influence has been diminished. The consequence of this paradox has been an emphasis on the headteacher as manager rather than as educationalist. This shift in emphasis has exposed headteachers to the full blast of managerialism, which has its own particular blend of exhortation and incantation, expressed in a vocabulary more in tune with factory production than the education of young children. School leadership has been reduced to a series of disconnected skills and abilities focused upon resource management, development planning and the pursuit of so-called efficiency and effectiveness.

It is our belief that this is an inadequate account of what it means to be a headteacher. We believe that as leaders of schools, headteachers' responsibilities are not adequately defined in terms of efficiency and effectiveness, but require a more thoughtful account which focuses upon the particular nature of educational leadership. We are not disputing the importance of the quality of educational leadership to a school, but we do believe that the nature of the leadership must be rooted in the values of educational discourse rather than those of the market place.

We have argued that educational leadership should be embracing and inclusive, and that it should strive to uphold democratic ideals, that it should be educative, ethical, critical and transformative. We have tried to give some idea of what this might mean in practice. To adopt such a stance as a headteacher you will need enormous strength, determination and stamina. But perhaps most importantly you will need confidence and self-belief. These are not comfortable times to be a headteacher, but it is precisely because of the pressures and uncertainties of the time that the need for steadfast school leadership is so great.

To undertake the job of headteacher is to accept a profoundly important responsibility. To model successfully what it might mean to be educated is a challenge worthy of the very best of our teachers. Headship still remains a job which is capable of offering enormous satisfaction and which has the potential to make a huge difference to people's lives.

We believe passionately that headteachers should receive training and support. The opportunity presented by the TTA initiative to provide headteachers with a national qualification is an important step forward. It is important that the training places sufficient emphasis upon the nature of educational leadership, as we have defined it, rather than the off-the-shelf management training manuals. It is, in our view, important that headteachers are recruited from the best of the teaching profession and that they are encouraged to reflect upon the values, attitudes and skills they held and employed in the classroom when considering how they might set about the job of headteacher.

BIBLIOGRAPHY

ACE (1995) *Governors' Handbook*. London: Advisory Centre for Education.

ACSTT/INIST (1976) *Towards a National Policy for the Induction and In-service Training of Teachers in Schools*. London: ACSTT/INIST.

ACSTT/INIST (1978) *Making INSET Work*. London: HMSO.

Ainscow, M. and Hopkins, D. (1994) Understanding the moving school. In G. Southworth (ed.) *Readings in Primary School Development*. London: Falmer Press.

Angus, L. (1989) 'New leadership' and the possibility of educational reform. In J. Smyth (ed.) *Critical Perspectives on Educational Leadership*. Lewes: Falmer Press.

Barnes, C. (1993) *Practical Marketing for Schools*. Oxford: Blackwell Business.

Bennett, N. (1997) *Teaching Styles and Pupil Progress*. London: Open Books.

Bennis, W. (1989) Managing the dream: leadership in the 21st century, *Journal of Organisational Change Management*, 2(1).

Block, P. (1987) *The Empowered Manager*. San Francisco: Jossey Bass.

Burns, J.M. (1978) *Leadership*. New York: Harper and Row.

Callaghan, J. (1976) Text of Ruskin College speech, *Times Educational Supplement*, 22 October.

Carr, W. (1995) *For Education*. Buckingham: Open University Press.

CEDC (1993) *Parents as Co-educators*. Coventry: Community Education Development Centre.

Codd, J. (1989) Educational leadership as reflective action. In J. Smyth (ed.) *Critical Perspectives on Educational Leadership*. Lewes: Falmer Press.

Coulson, A. (1974) The role of the primary head. In C. Richards (ed.) *The Study of Primary Education: a Source Book, Volume 3*. Lewes: Falmer Press.

Craig, I. (ed.) (1989) *Primary Headship in the 1990s*. Harlow: Longman.

Day, C., Hall, C., Gammage, P. and Coles, M. (1993) *Leadership and Curriculum in the Primary School. The Role of Senior and Middle Management*. London: Paul Chapman Publishing.

Day, C., Whitaker, P. and Johnston, D. (1990) *Managing Primary Schools in the 1990s: a Professional Development Approach*. London: Paul Chapman Publishing.

Deal, T.E. (1987) The culture of schools. In L.T. Sheive and M.B. Schoenheit (eds) *Leadership: Examining the Elusive*. Arlington, VA: Association for Supervision and Curriculum Development.

DES (1972) *Teacher Education and Training*. London: HMSO.

DES (1977) *A New Partnership for Our Schools*. London: HMSO.

DES (1979) *Local Authority Arrangements for the School Curriculum: Report of the Circular 14/77 Review*. London: HMSO.

DES (1981) *The School Curriculum*. London: HMSO.

DES (1985) *Better Schools*. London: HMSO.

DES (1990) *Developing School Management: the Way Forward*. London: HMSO.

DES (1991) *Development Planning: a Practical Guide*. London: HMSO.

DES (1992) *Curriculum Organisation and Classroom Practice in Primary Schools*. London: HMSO.

Ferguson, K. (1984) *The Feminist Case against Bureaucracy*. Philadelphia: Temple University Press.

Foster, W. (1989) Towards a critical practice of leadership. In J. Smyth (ed.) *Critical Perspectives on Educational Leadership*. Lewes: Falmer Press.

Fullan, M. (1991) *The New Meaning of Educational Change*. New York: Teachers Educational Press.

Fullan, M. (1992) *What's Worth Fighting for in Headship*. Buckingham: Open University Press.

Fullan, M. (1993) *Changing Forces: Probing the Depths of Educational Reform*. London: Falmer Press.

Glatter, R., Preedy, M., Riches, C. and Masterton, M. (1988) *Understanding School Management*. Milton Keynes: Open University Press.

Grace, G. (1995) *School Leadership: Beyond Education Management*. Lewes: Falmer Press.

Handy, C. (1994) *The Empty Raincoat*. London: Random House.

Hargreaves, D. and Hopkins, D. (1991) *The Empowered School*. London: Cassell.

Hargreaves, D., Hopkins, D., Leash, M., Connolly, J. and Robinson, P. (1989) *Planning for School Development. Advice to Governors, Headteachers and Teachers*. London: HMSO.

Harrison, M. and Gill, S. (1992) *Primary School Management*. Oxford: Heinemann.

HMI (1978) *Primary Education in England: a Survey by HM Inspectors of Schools*. London: HMSO.

Hodgkinson, C. (1978) *Towards a Philosophy of Administration*. Oxford: Basil Blackwell.

Holly, P. (1987) Making it count: evaluation for the developing primary school. In G. Southworth (ed.) *Readings in Primary School Management*. London: Falmer Press.

House of Commons Education, Science and Arts Committee (1986) *Achievement in Primary Schools*. London: HMSO.

Hughes, M., Wikeley, F. and Nash, T. (1990) *Parents on the National Curriculum: an Interim Report*. Exeter: University of Exeter.

Hutton, W. (1995) *The State We're In*. London: Jonathan Cape.

ILEA (1982) *Keeping the School under Review*. London: ILEA.

ILEA (1985) *Improving Primary Schools*. London: ILEA.

Inglis, F. (1989) Managerialism and morality: the corporate and the republican school. In W. Carr (ed.) *Quality in Teaching*. Lewes: Falmer Press.

Jowett, S., Bajinsky, M. and MacNeil-MacDonald, M. (1991) *Building Bridges*. Slough: NFER-Nelson.

Luttwark, E. (1994) Why fascism is the wave of the future, *London Review of Books*, 7 April.

MacGilchrist, B., Mortimore, P., Savage, J. and Beresford, C. (1995) *Planning Matters. The Impact of Development Planning in Primary Schools*. London: Paul Chapman Publishing.

McIntyre, A. (1985) *After Virtue*. London: Duckworth.

Maclure, S. (1988) *Education Reformed*. London: Hodder and Stoughton.

McMahon, A., Bolam, R., Abbot, R. and Holly, P. (1984) *Guidelines for Review and Internal Development in Schools: Primary School Handbook*. York: Longman/SCDC.

Marr, A. (1995) *Ruling Britannia*. London: Michael Joseph.

Mortimore, P., Sammons, P., Stoll, S., Lewis, D. and Ecob, R. (1988) *School Matters*. Wells: Open Books.

National Commission on Education (1995) *Success against the Odds: Effective Schools in Disadvantaged Areas*. London: Routledge.

Nias, J. (1989) *Primary Teachers Talking: a Study of Teaching as Work*. London: Routledge.

Nias, J., Southworth, G. and Campbell, P. (1992) *Whole School Curriculum Development in the Primary School*. London: Falmer Press.

Nias, J., Southworth, G. and Yeomans, R. (1989) *Staff Relationships in the Primary School: a Study for Organizational Cultures*. London: Cassell.

Ofsted (1994) *The Annual Report of Her Majesty's Chief Inspector of Schools Part 1*. London: HMSO.

Peters, R.S. (ed.) (1976) *The Role of the Head*. London: Routledge.

Peters, T. (1989) *Thriving on Chaos: Handbook for a Management Revolution*. London: Pan.

Peters, T. and Waterman, R. Jr (1982) *In Search of Excellence*. London: HarperCollins.

Reynolds, D. and Parker, A. (1992) School effectiveness and school improvement in the 1990s. In D. Reynolds and P. Cutlance (eds) *School Effectiveness: Research Theory and Practice*. London: Cassell.

Rivzi, F. (1989) Bureaucratic rationality and the promise of democratic schooling. In W. Carr (ed.) *Quality in Teaching*. Lewes: Falmer Press.

Schön, D.A. (1983) *The Reflective Practitioner*. London: Temple South.

Southworth, G. (1995) *Looking into Primary Headship: a Research Based Interpretation*. Lewes: Falmer Press.

Starratt, R.J. (1990) *The Drama of Schooling – the Schooling of Drama*. Lewes: Falmer Press.

Stoll, L. and Fink, D. (1996) *Changing Our Schools*. Buckingham: Open University Press.

Street-Porter, J. (1995) Snagged by men in suits, *The Guardian*, 26 August.

Waters, D. (1979) *Management and Headship in the Primary School*. London: Ward Lock.

Webb, R. and Vulliamy, G. (1996) *Roles and Responsibilities in the Primary School*. Buckingham: Open University Press.

Woodhead, C. (1995) Education: the elusive engagement and the continuing frustration, annual lecture, Royal Society of Arts, London, January.

CHANGING OUR SCHOOLS

Louise Stoll and Dean Fink

Many of our schools are good schools – if this were 1965. Processes and structures designed for a time that has passed are no longer appropriate in a rapidly changing society. Throughout the world a great deal of effort and money has been expended in the name of educational change. Much of it has been misdirected and some of it wasteful. This book assists people inside and outside schools to bring about positive change by helping them to define the purposes behind change, the processes needed to achieve change and the results which they should expect. By linking the **why**, **what** and **how** of change, the authors provide both a theoretical critique and practical advice to assist all those committed to changing and improving schools.

> Very few books on school reform contain so many ideas and insights while managing to construct a coherent and comprehensive message. Stoll and Fink have written an invaluable resource which is rich both conceptually and practically. This is a book that can be read in part or whole with great profit.
>
> Michael Fullan

Contents

Good schools if this were 1965: the context of change – The Halton Effective Schools Project: a story of change – School effectiveness can inform school improvement – The possibilities and challenges of school improvement – School development planning: a path to change – The power of school culture – Invitational leadership – Changing concepts of teaching and learning – The need for partnerships – Learning for all: building the learning community – Evaluate what you value – Changing our schools: linking school effectiveness and school improvement – References – Index.

240pp   0 335 19290 4 (paperback)   0 335 19291 2 (hardback)

WHAT'S WORTH FIGHTING FOR IN YOUR SCHOOL?
WORKING TOGETHER FOR IMPROVEMENT

Michael Fullan and Andy Hargreaves

This is about how to make schools more interesting and fulfilling places to be. It tackles how to bring about marked improvements in the daily lives and experiences of teachers, heads and pupils. The premise is that teachers and heads themselves should ultimately *make* this happen.

Almost everywhere, teachers and heads are overloaded and undervalued. Teachers and heads will need to take more of the initiative themselves, not just in holding off unreasonable demands, not just in bargaining for better conditions but also in making constructive improvements of their own, as a professional community. Examples of such constructive practice already exist but they need to be broadened, strengthened and developed. This book is meant to stimulate such improvements. It is a practical book and a provocative one; fully aware of the constraints and everyday problems facing teachers but clear in setting out what really is worth fighting for in schools.

No teacher or head will read this book without responding in the light of his or her personal experiences, beliefs and passion about teaching; and all will be challenged by this catalyst for action.

Contents
Preface to the British edition – Foreword – Acknowledgements – The authors – Introduction – The problem – Total teachers – Total schools – Guidelines for action – References.

160pp   0 335 15755 6 (paperback)

ROLES AND RESPONSIBILITIES IN THE PRIMARY SCHOOL
CHANGING DEMANDS, CHANGING PRACTICES

Rosemary Webb and Graham Vulliamy

♦ How are teachers planning and implementing the National Curriculum at Key Stage 2?
♦ How have the recent policy and legislative changes affected the roles and responsibilities of class teachers, curriculum coordinators, deputy head-teachers and headteachers?
♦ How are primary schools managing the current plethora of innovations and what can be learned from their experience?

Based on qualitative research in 50 schools throughout England and Wales, this book portrays teachers' work as it is currently experienced in the post-ERA context of multiple innovations. It examines the impact of the National Curriculum and assessment on classroom practice, curriculum organization and planning at Key Stage 2. Drawing on the wealth of ideas and successful practices shared with the authors by the teachers in the study, it demonstrates how classteachers, curriculum coordinators, deputy headteachers and headteachers are tackling the new demands of their expanding roles. An analysis of the management of change reveals a growing tension between collegial and top-down directive managerial styles, which is fundamentally affecting the culture of primary schools. Through presenting what is actually happening in primary schools in contrast to prescribed educational ortho-doxies, this book makes a vital contribution to the debate on the future of primary education.

Contents
Introduction and methodology – The changing context of primary education – Changing demands on classroom practice – Changing curriculum organization and planning – The changing role of the curriculum coordinator – The changing role of the deputy headteacher – The changing role of the headteacher – Managing whole school change in the post-ERA primary school – References – Index.

192pp   0 335 19472 9 (paperback)   0 335 19473 7 (hardback)

308046